MICHAEL L. PAPESH

The Listening Parish

A GUIDEBOOK TO SYNODALITY PRACTICES IN A FAITH COMMUNITY

✴ The Pastoral Center

Dedicated

to the theologians of the Roman Catholic Church

East and West:

in hope for the development

of a vibrant, penetrating, accessible theology of Trinity,

a theology of the Holy Spirit

fired with discernment and breathing of trust,

and a compelling theology of the Church as family ...

so we might ever more confidently travel together

— minds convinced, hearts free,

eyes delighted, and ears open —

in one vast, complex, listening, searching,

discerning, united and joyful communion

on the synodal way.

Copyright © 2023 Michael L. Papesh. All rights reserved. No part of this publication may be reproduced in any manner without the prior written approval of the author and publisher. Published by The Pastoral Center/PastoralCenter.com. Please contact us to purchase a parish reprint license and electronic access to the content.

The Scripture passages contained herein are from the New Revised Standard Version of the Bible, copyright © 1989, by the Division of Christian Education of the National Council of Churches in the U.S.A. All rights reserved.

ISBN 978-1-949628-30-2

Contents

A. Introduction 5
   1. Using This Guidebook 7
   2. On Being Family 9
   3. Assumptions Exposed 11

B. Considering Synodality 13
   1. What is the Call About? 15
   2. Reflection Questions 17
   3. What is Synodality? 19
   4. A Case Study 21
   5. A Dynamic Model of Church 23
   6. Co-Responsibility & Respect ... 25
   7. Beliefs Grounding Synodality . 27
   8. What Synodality is Not 29
   9. Thought-Provoking Images 31

C. The Synodal Path for the Parish .. 33
   1. Probing Practices Questions ... 35
   2. Parish Practices for the Journey .. 37

D. Church Structure 39
   1. The Diocese 41
   2. Parish Civil Law Status 43
   3. Parish and Leadership Variation .. 45

E. The Pastor 47
   1. The Parish and the Pastor 49
   2. What Pastoring Requires 51
   3. One Among Many 53
   4. Reflections for a Pastor 55

F. Council Basics 57
   1. Parish Councils in Law 59
   2. The Councils' Mission 61
   3. Planning and the Pastoral Council .. 63
   4. Planning and the Finance Council .. 65
   5. Council Election & Eligibility .. 67

G. Council Meetings 69
   1. Effective Council Meetings 71
   2. The Place of Confidentiality .. 73
   3. Meeting Agendas 75
   4. Meeting Mechanics 76
   5. Meeting Facilitation 77
   6. Who Chairs the Meeting? 79

H. Discernment Decision-Making ... 81
   1. Discerning Together 83
   2. A Sample Discernment Process .. 85
   3. Further Reflections 87

I. The Ministry Staff 89
   1. Staff Titles 91
   2. Decision-Making 93
   3. Communion in Co-Pastoring 95
   4. Commissions & Decision-Making . 97
   5. Administrative Staff 99

J. Parishes with Schools 101
   1. School As Parish Ministry 103
   2. The School Principal 105
   3. School Ministry Governance 107

K. Just Employment Practices **109**
    1. Synodality and Just Employment 111
    2. Covenant Ministry 113
    3. Ministry Planning & Review 115
    4. Covenant Hiring 117
    5. Just Compensation 119
    6. Just Termination 121

L. Building a Parish Assembly **123**
    1. Engaging the Parish Assembly 125
    2. Two Annual Reports 127
    3. A Sample Data Gathering 129

M. Moving Toward the Peripheries **131**
    1. Opening to the Peripheries 133
    2. Responding to the Peripheries 135
    3. A Large Group Listening Process 137

N. A Sample Pastoral Planning Process **139**
    1. Process Outline 141
    2. Step 1: Parish Sense of Self 143
    3. Sample Beliefs Statements 145
    4. Step 2: Parish Image 147
    5. Sample Organization Charts 149
    6. Step 3: Parish Direction 151
    7. Sample Goals & Objectives 153
    8. Steps 4-8. Parish Accomplishment ... 155

O. Parish Synodality in Practice **157**
    1. Living the Spirit of Synodality 159
    2. Some Limits 161
    3. Participating in God's Family Life ... 163

INTRODUCTION

INTRODUCTION

Using This Guidebook

"A SYNODAL CHURCH IS A LISTENING CHURCH..." —POPE FRANCIS

This work is designed for practical use within a parish. While it can certainly be read through in sequence by an individual ministry leader, it is also a toolkit that can be used in a targeted manner with groups.

Each chapter is formatted as a two-page handout so that it can be reproduced on a single sheet of paper. The digital "eResource" edition is licensed for use within a parish or diocesan office, allowing you to easily share one or more of these handouts with your leadership teams by email and/or as physical copies.

You may choose to distribute one or more handouts in advance of a meeting, so your participants can read them beforehand and discuss when you gather. Use whatever chapters are most helpful for your team and its current situation in whatever order you wish.

May the Holy Spirit guide your way as you journey together as church!

INTRODUCTION

On Being Family

The Aim

In the end, synodality is all about being family. Church as family. The Church united as family—one family, our family, in communion with the divine family that is the Trinity.

So What Is Family?

Catholics hold that the family is the first institution of, and foundation for, all human life. Created by God as God's masterpiece, a mirror of God's life as Father, Son, and Holy Spirit, Catholics understand that the family serves as the seedbed for life itself. A privileged community comprised of members who are persons complementary yet equal in dignity, family also "consists in sharing relationships of faithful love, trust, cooperation, reciprocity" (Pope Francis) that bring about happiness for each member.

> The family humanizes people through the relationship of "we" and at the same time promotes each person's legitimate differences.
>
> Pope Francis, April 29, 2022

A community of faith, hope, and love, the family aims to nurture and protect life, offer support and security for healthy growth into full humanity, stimulate vibrant faith in God, and bathe its members all the while in unconditional love.

Indeed, as the Catholic Church understands it, the family serves humans as the ground experience of justice. Family is the womb for the birth of reverent human freedom, abiding human security, and an expansive and tender fulfillment of human needs.

> The relationships within the family bring an affinity of feelings, affections, and interests, arising above all from the members' respect for one another.
>
> *Catechism of the Catholic Church*, 2206

Reality Straining Toward the Ideal

Growing up in an extended Catholic family, I was told that family was the secure place where my needs could be met, that family members were the people I could trust, and that family was the only sure, safe harbor for life.

My mother and father ended their marriage when I was 23, away in seminary. Their surprise divorce and subsequent remarriages within two years heaped a great trauma on me, which would scratch, scrape, and sear for the next 35 years.

When my family shattered, I sought substitutes in other families, friendships, "priestly fraternity," and faith community life. At the same time, I continued to pursue an authentic experience of family—as best I could—through relentless attempts for right relationship as I strove to honor my father and mother, their new partners, and their changed contexts and lives, as well as in my broader family life, all amidst the shards.

In the end, failing to find family's promise in my own family, I found it in two other places.

First, I found fulfillment through searching for and striving to surrender to life and love within and among the Father, the Son, and the Holy Spirit as Trinity—the divine family of the Three in One and One in Three.

> You called, you shouted, and you broke through my deafness. You flashed, you shone, and you dispelled my blindness. You breathed your fragrance on me; I drew in breath and now I pant for you. I have tasted you, now I hunger and thirst for more. You touched me, and I burned for your peace.
>
> St. Augustine, *Confessions*

Always a sinner and ever a clumsy partner within the divine dance, I found tender mercy and the restoration of the joy of my youth through accepting, surrendering to, and abiding within the unfathomable mystery of relating with God explicitly as Trinity.

My second experience of family fulfillment came in striving for the gift of consensus in ministry decision-making. I made plenty of missteps and mistakes. Nonetheless, working to enter fully into this process with college students or parishioners in leadership, with parish staffs in planning, or with fellow priests in council offered me the shared relationships of faithful love, trust, cooperation, and reciprocity that fleshed out what I lost and lacked in my family life.

Within these processes and relationships, gradually, over the years, I became a true believer in prayer and what Pope Francis calls "the practices of synodality."

> Becoming a disciple of Jesus means accepting the invitation to belong to God's family, to live in conformity with [God's] way of life: 'for whoever does the will of my Father in heaven is my brother, and sister, and mother.'
>
> *Catechism of the Catholic Church*, 2233

The Vision Synodality Offers: Church as Family

From the beginning, prostitutes and sinners, the poor, outcasts, and the alienated comprise the searchers who, filled with deep and sometimes unarticulated longing, seek the experience of family within the embrace of Christian faith community life. The Acts of the Apostles and the letters of Paul illustrate the struggles that ensue, as well as the values and dispositions required, as we journey together toward that fulfillment of the family of faith's—the Church's—promise.

This family theme has remained throughout our history. Over the centuries, the Western Church evolved the custom of placing a shrine to the Blessed Virgin Mary on one side of the church assembly building and a shrine to St. Joseph on the other, the Blessed Sacrament reposed in the middle. This devotional placement strongly suggested the church as Nazareth; the parish as a place of respite and rest, deepening relationship and security, comfort, growth, and joy; our community as family.

In 1995, Pope John Paul II's apostolic exhortation *Ecclesia in Africa* offered the image of the Church as the family of God. This model of Church, the Pope proposed, arising from within a critically important Church within our universal communion, serves as a particularly appropriate expression of the nature of the Church, underlining as it does the Church's notes of community spirit, solidarity, solicitude, generosity, and hospitality.

The Promise of Being Family

The promise of Church as a pilgrim family on the way to God includes within it the roly-poly, pell-mell, tumble-bumble of all human family life. We saw that among the disciples and within the early communities. We see it vividly today in our parishes, dioceses, national churches, and the Synod on Synodality.

At the same time, the synodal practices offered in what follows—listening and sharing honestly of our experience and ideas; engaging in relationships of faithful love, trust, cooperation, and reciprocity; striving for consensus about what God wants of us in our community's decision-making and decision taking—aim to extend a familial hope.

Implemented in the parish, these synodality practices invite us to reverence and mirror in our parish life the dance of the Trinity's life and the dance of our own families within the life of the Church. These practices aim to embody for the parish Pope Francis' call to enter into the promise and pilgrimage of becoming, as Church, the universal family of God. ∎

INTRODUCTION

Assumptions Exposed

The Aim

Pope Francis has invited the universal Church to walk the path toward synodality:

> Synodality is a style; it is a walk together, and it is what the Lord expects from the Church of the third millennium.
>
> Pope Francis, November 29, 2019

This work offers practical ideas, guidelines, and tools for implementing synodality practices in the parish. What follows rests on six assumptions.

Synodality is Ancient Yet Unfamiliar

The first assumption is that synodality is new to us.

The practice of holding Church synods is ancient. The so-called Council of Jerusalem in the year 50 (Acts of the Apostles, Chapter 15) is often cited as the first Church synod. It was not called that at the time, but during the third quarter of the second century, the Church began using the word synod for gatherings of multiple churches to discuss problems.

Over the centuries, the use of the term synod has varied, and synods have taken different forms—sometimes bishops, presbyters, and laity met; sometimes bishops and presbyters; sometimes bishops only. Many in the Church today, therefore, may be unacquainted with the term or feel fuzzy about its meaning.

A Parish Cannot Hold a Synod

Strictly speaking, a synod is an assembly of the pastoral leaders of churches gathered to discuss matters of concern, often matters of disagreement. Synods may be a universal gathering, a regional gathering, or a diocesan gathering of churches.

> [The parish] is a community of communities, a sanctuary where the thirsty come to drink in the midst of their journey, and a center of constant missionary outreach.
>
> Pope Francis, *The Joy of the Gospel*, 28

While the parish is a community of communities, it is but a single church. Consequently, a parish cannot be or hold a synod.

The Parish is Synodality's Seedbed

However, a third assumption is that a vibrant parish community expresses its life through attitudes and practices critical for the larger Church that would be considered synodal. That is, a vital parish nurtures practices of synodality in its style of being Church.

What might a synodal-minded parish look like?

❋ Humbly inclusive pastoring

❋ Consensus-building parish council processes

THE LISTENING PARISH

- A collegial ministry staff
- Regular and careful listening to the people
- Wide invitations for parishioner participation in pastoral leadership and ministry
- Discernment decision-making as commonplace
- Accountability
- Transparency
- Just organizational practices
- Relationship and ministry movement toward the poor and those on the peripheries of the parish and life

All these parish practices are synodality notes in themselves and serve synodality in the larger Church. When a parish embraces a synodal style and implements synodal procedures, it inspires and serves as a training ground for the larger Church to be authentically itself and synodal in the Gospel mission.

The Larger Church is the Synodal Focus Now

The great work of journeying together on the synodal path currently preoccupies the Church's universal, continental, and national levels. Participation in nurturing synodal practice on these levels is a critical focus in our time. That is as it should be.

However elemental to the Church's life, the parish as an engine of synodality currently sits on the back burner as the larger Church does its building work.

Still, the Parish is Crucial to Becoming a Synodal Church

A fifth assumption is that we know enough about the call to synodality to explore what its notes need to look like on a parish level.

Let's Explore How to Nurture Synodal Practice in the Parish

What follows, therefore, is a work of coaching. It seeks to offer ideas, guidelines, and tools for parishes that desire to better express synodality practices. This work seeks:

- to point out what is necessary for a parish to embrace a synodal style
- to assist a parish in blessing what synodal notes already exist in its life, and
- to offer suggestions and pointers to help a parish refine and further develop synodality practices.

> The renewal of structures demanded by pastoral conversion can only be understood in this light: as part of an effort to make them more mission-oriented, to make ordinary pastoral activity on every level more inclusive and open, to inspire in pastoral workers a constant desire to go forth and in this way to elicit a positive response from all those whom Jesus summons to friendship with him.
>
> Pope Francis, *The Joy of the Gospel*, 27

We Are On a Journey

The final assumption is that we, as Church, are on a path of great experiment.

This work of coaching, therefore, remains humble. It aims simply to underscore the importance of certain sound practices, offer some food for thought, and encourage pastoral leaders to creative responses in their own parish to the call of the deepening our pastoral impulse to effective Gospel mission.

CONSIDERING SYNODALITY

CONSIDERING SYNODALITY

What is the Call About?

The Church: Always Reforming

Like creation, the universal Church groans in one great act of giving birth to new life in Christ Jesus for all peoples (Romans 8:22).

Christianity is eternal. Its forms, however, are linked to history and conditioned by given stages of development. Faithfulness to our mission as Church requires adaptation in every age.

Spreading the message of Jesus Christ and the pattern of life he has shown us demands that in every age, the Church rethink its ways of being and operating, which includes the Church's

* functions
* governance
* modes of participation
* and structures of accountability.

As Pope St. Paul VI stated when he opened the second session of Vatican II in 1963, this reforming task presupposes "the desire, the need, and the duty of the Church finally to provide a more complete definition of itself."

> The Second Vatican Council presented ecclesial conversion as an openness to constant self-renewal born of fidelity to Jesus Christ… Christ summons the Church, as she goes her pilgrim way…to that continual reformation of which she always had need.
>
> Pope Francis, *Joy of the Gospel* 26

Faithfulness to the Gospel calls us all as Church to a constant process of growth and renewal, to permanent conversion and purification, if we are to remain faithful.

The First Aim of the Call

Pope Francis calls us to synodality to help make our mission as Church in our time more dynamic and effective.

> All renewal in the Church must have mission as its goal if it is not to fall prey to a kind of ecclesial introversion.
>
> Pope Francis, *Joy of the Gospel* 27

The first aim of the call to synodality is to invite the whole Church to channel our customs, ways of doing things, times, schedules, language, and structures for "evangelization of today's world rather than for (the Church's) institutional preservation" (*Joy of the Gospel* 27). This invitation calls us to a new mindset as Church, sending us to the peripheries to listen to real human needs, then returning to the center to discern how we as Church reestablish communion with all people at all levels so we might all become one people of God.

THE LISTENING PARISH

To accomplish this end, synodality as a style and mindset seeks to build forms of listening, discernment, dialogue, and decision-making that strengthen the bonds of unity among the successor of Peter, the bishops, the ordained, and all the faithful in Christ, all of whom share co-responsibility for the Church's mission.

Other Aims of the Call

Today, we stand as a clerical, authoritarian Church unsettled by conflict. Our sociological structures have served us well in ages past; they grew out of historical necessity. But clericalism today—"the complex of being chosen," as Pope Francis calls it—has become a systemic weakness because clerical culture has become monarchical in practice and socially stratified.

The clerical sex abuse scandal and scandal of the widespread lack of financial accountability are the shocking tip of the iceberg for the Church.

Clericalism thrives when service is confused with power. This creates in the Church an authoritarian style, a hierarchical worldview, and the tendency to identify holiness and grace with the clerical state. These social dynamics distort the cleric's power over persons and the hierarchy's power over the people of God. They lead to what Pope Francis listed in his December 22, 2014, Christmas address to the Curia as "unhealthy elements that need reform":

* neglect of controls
* excessive planning and functionalism
* loss of communion among the Church's members
* extravagant garments and honors
* careerism and opportunism
* membership in closed circles.

These unhealthy elements exclude and divide in the Church, separating us rather than uniting us for mission.

What the Church Needs Today

To counteract these unhealthy movements and their hobbling us in mission, we need a change of mindset.

In this third millennium, we as Church can now create structures of participation which situate the primacy of the successor of Peter within the college of bishops and the collegial decision-making of the bishops and clergy within the whole people of God.

We as a Church could today become a community of free and open persons who cooperate responsibly, united in solidarity, participating together responsibly and with accountability in the Church's mission.

We could create a mindset and structures of participation that express the universal baptismal commission to mission.

In our time, for the sake of the mission's effectiveness, we could embrace being Church as a genuine "we":

* all the baptized equal before God
* all in communion together as the faithful in Christ
* all sharing the same responsibility, in accord with our stations and gifts, for our identity, vocation, and mission as Church.

Achieving this change of mindset and style as a universal Church is no small task. We have many obstacles to overcome.

And our becoming a genuine, universal "we" as Church begins in the parish.

CONSIDERING SYNODALITY

Reflection Questions

WHAT IS THE IMPACT OF SCANDAL?

* How has your experience of Church or feelings about the Church been touched or changed by the clerical sex abuse crisis?
* What positive changes have you witnessed in the parish because of pastoral leadership or community sensitivities that grew out of the experience of the scandal?
* How would you rate your parish's accountability regarding its finances (1 being completely opaque and 10 being completely transparent)?
* What mechanisms of financial accountability seem to work best for the parish?

PARISH COUNCIL LEADERSHIP

* Does your parish have a pastoral council?
* How engaged is your parish's pastoral council in shaping the parish's life, especially its ministry planning and implementation (1 being completely disengaged and 10 being completely engaged)?
* Does your parish have a finance council?
* How engaged is your parish finance council in preparing and monitoring the budget and managing the parish's property assets (1 being completely disengaged and 10 being completely engaged)?
* How are the parish pastoral and finance council members selected?
* What within your parish's experience of councils seems to work most smoothly and well?

GENERAL LEADERSHIP MATTERS

* To what extent is the whole parish community solicited and engaged in dialogue about pastoral leadership (1 being not at all solicited and engaged and 10 being consistently solicited and engaged)?
* What mechanisms and processes are used in the parish to solicit opinions and engage everyone to discern leadership concerns?
* What mechanisms and processes seem to work best?
* What forums and ways of proceeding exist in the parish so community members may freely offer advice, process their concerns, discuss larger Church issues, or resolve community conflicts?
* What forums or ways of proceeding have proven most productive?
* Who or what groups hold effective power—the capacity to achieve a common purpose—in the parish?
* Who or what groups hold power in a particularly notable segment or area of parish life?
* Who or what persons or groups are excluded from power in the parish?
* Who or what groups in the parish are ignored or overlooked by parish leadership?
* Is pastoral leadership accountable to the parish community?
* How is pastoral leadership held accountable?
* Are some in pastoral leadership more accountable than others and how is that expressed?

CONSIDERING SYNODALITY

What is Synodality?

The Meaning of the Word

Synod comes from the Greek *syn*, together, and *hodos*, way: walking together. Used in the Church since the third century, *synod* refers to regional assemblies of bishops and diocesan assemblies of clergy who gather to discuss matters of doctrine and practice. Vatican II was a form of synod.

Regarding bishops' meetings, the words *synod* and *council* have tended to be used interchangeably. Larger assemblies of bishops have favored the word *council*.

Pope Francis calls us to understand *synodality* far beyond the convening of events. He invites us to synodality as a mindset and style that governs all we are and do as Church. He calls us to be Church in a way that sets in motion constant transformation: all the baptized striving together, sharing co-responsibility for bringing the Gospel to the world, joining together in a permanent state of Gospel mission.

> The path of synodality is the path that God expects of the Church of the third millennium. What the Lord asks of us is already contained, in a sense, in the word "synod," which means "walking together"—laity, pastors, Bishop of Rome.
>
> Pope Francis, October 17, 2015

A synodal Church goes out to the peripheries to listen to people's real needs, brings the results of listening back to the community, and then structures processes for the whole community to discern the meaning of what was heard and how the Church might respond. Pastors and people together, in this framework, fashion and implement a response that proclaims the Gospel, expands communion in the Church, and accompanies people in helping meet their real needs.

Listening and Discerning Together

> A synodal Church is a Church that listens, which realizes that listening is more than simply hearing. It is mutual listening in which everyone has something to learn. The faithful people, the college of bishops, the bishop of Rome all listening to each other, all listening to the Holy Spirit, the Spirit of Truth.
>
> Pope Francis, October 17, 2015

Pope Francis proposes that listening, dialoguing, and discerning together characterize the dynamic process of interaction and communion that is being Church. Listening opens us to being changed in our identity and relationships, our ears tuned to one another in a horizontal dynamic, all listening together, people and pastors, so we can know what the Spirit is saying to the churches (Revelation 2:7).

The act of listening leads us into becoming a culture of en-

THE LISTENING PARISH   19

counter and accompaniment in a permanent state of mission.

Listening to the signs of the times draws us into updating and renewing the foundational event of Christianity. Through reciprocal listening relationships, we allow ourselves to be impacted not simply by doctrine and customs but also by the on-the-ground culture of our time, the context in which Gospel mission takes place today.

Co-Responsibility in Mission

A fuller implementation of synodality summons us to rethink the Church's mission so we might better shape how we fulfill it in our time. Two keys, especially, must be kept in mind for following the synodal way.

First, proceeding together in mission requires that the whole community gather so that it might pray, listen, analyze, dialogue, and offer advice for the sake of pastoral

* planning
* decision-making
* decision-taking
* and implementation.

Proceeding together rests on the principled conviction that what affects everyone in the Church community must be discussed and approved by everyone.

Second, accepting co-responsibility means that we strive for the effective participation of all according to each one's calling because all are qualified to reflect on the mission, and all are called to serve. Effectiveness for mission demands that we achieve unity in plurality and come to the whole through and with all the parts.

Becoming a Dynamic Church

The call to synodality invites us to encounter and accompany one another, especially in conflict.

The synodal way invites us to engage different viewpoints face-to-face in an environment and with a method of discernment. It calls us to express and listen with openness to learning new ways of seeing and valuing, which might lead us to find links to new and more effective structures and channels for being Church that are more closely aligned with the Gospel.

Walking the synodal path means that the totality of the faithful—pastors and people together in horizontal relationship—make the decisions that shape Gospel mission in our time. This process demands that we find methods and ways to help the faith community achieve consensus about our mission. And since building consensus requires that we discern together not simply ours but the Holy Spirit's truth about our missionary path, consensus decisions must be binding for all—pastors and people together.

Consequently, becoming a synodal Church requires that we find effective ways for listening, discerning, dialoguing, and co-sharing—the capacity to achieve purpose for the common good of all. This necessity invites us to create relational dynamics, a human environment, and accountability practices for effective consensus building:

* reciprocal listening
* exchanging and communicating
* sharing and growing in solidarity
* the desire to reach consensus
* and coming to a common conviction.

A synodal spirit demands a new kind of collaboration, cooperation, acceptance, welcome, giving, and receiving—pastors and people accompanying one another—within our life together as Church.

Building the dynamics of synodality as a way of being Church will take creativity and wisdom. Growing in the mindset and style of synodality demands experimenting. Our intent on the journey is simply to better be Church in our time: abiding in mission relationships steeped in respect and charity, humility, and justice, open to ongoing conversion of heart, and reaching for constant purification by the Holy Spirit whom we encounter in our listening and discernment.

CONSIDERING SYNODALITY

A Case Study

The Facts on the Ground

The Diocese of Rustburg established Light of Christ parish in 1960 on Rustburg's expanding north side. A middle-class, blue-collar, and economically stagnant town today, Rustburg grew out of the 19th-century engines of coal mining, steel mills, and railroad freight transportation. The decline of these industries in the last quarter of the 20th century left Rustburg's economy floundering.

When the state legalized marijuana, economically depressed people from surrounding states flocked to Rustburg to take advantage of its mild climate, cheap living, easy drug access, and lax police enforcement. Over time, this influx led to a housing shortage in Rustburg and a growing population of homeless people. This city of 112,000 estimates that over 300 people live on its streets today.

Though Light of Christ parish includes tony neighborhoods of university professors and administrators, doctors, lawyers, and other professionals, a wide creek runs north to south through the west side of the parish's territory, and intersects downtown. The length of the creek bed accommodates a hidden city where an estimated 200 tents shelter homeless men, women, and families, many of whom likely have mental illness, addiction, and poverty. The creek bed, hidden by homes and trees, sits five blocks from the Light of Christ parish complex.

Some Reflection Questions

❋ Does the Light of Christ community have any obligation to encounter, strive to accompany, and help meet the needs of the hundreds of homeless people who live within its boundaries?

❋ If Light of Christ community members were to go out to the peripheries, to the people living in this creek bed within its territory, what would they do there?

❋ What assemblies and processes need to be established so pastoral leaders and parishioners together might fashion and implement an accompanying response to the homeless among them that proclaims the Gospel, expands encounter and communion in the Church, and accompanies people to meet their real needs?

❋ How might the experience of the outreach be brought back to the parish?

❋ How might that be processed in the community?

❋ What might accountability to the parish and the homeless look like?

❋ What methods might be set up for ongoing encounter, dialogue, and accompaniment among the homeless and parish members? ■

CONSIDERING SYNODALITY

A Dynamic Model of Church

The People of God

The bishops gathered for Vatican II embraced a new orientation for the Church when they approved the document *Lumen Gentium* on November 21, 1964. After extended debate, the bishops chose a telling outline for the first chapters of *The Dogmatic Constitution on the Church*:

❋ The Mystery of the Church

❋ The People of God

❋ The Church is Hierarchical

❋ The Laity

❋ The Call to Holiness

For centuries, the Church, conceived as "a perfect society," had stoutly emphasized its hierarchical nature and authority structure. *Lumen Gentium's* structure reshaped the Church's vision of itself.

The Lumen Gentium Vision

Lumen Gentium embraced the image of the Church as the people of God, offering two fresh emphases.

First, the Church became understood as a single reality constituted by baptism.

❋ All in the Church are united with each other.

❋ All have the same fundamental laws and duties.

❋ All participate in Christ's royal priesthood.

❋ All—pope, bishops, priests, religious, laity—are the *Christifideles*, the faithful of Christ.

Second, because all members of the Church share baptism, we are all co-responsible for the Church's mission to teach, govern, and sanctify.

> The people of God is incarnate in the people of the earth, each of which has its own culture.
>
> Pope Francis, *Joy of the Gospel* 111

The Two Biblical Images

The *Lumen Gentium* image of the Church hearkens back to two biblical images.

One, from the Old Testament, is the pilgrim people of Israel journeying through the desert. The Church is a chosen people on a pilgrimage from slavery to freedom and promise.

The other image is the disciples of Christ. We, the Church, are disciples gathered around Jesus to share his life and to be sent forth into the world to preach the Good News.

Note: Both images—pilgrimage and gathering/going forth—are *dynamic*.

The Christifideles

The word Vatican II used to describe the whole people of God and, implicitly, the dynamic effects of baptism is *Christifideles*. This term stresses relationship, the immediate relationship of each and all the baptized with Jesus Christ and one another.

Each of the *Christifideles* finds their definition in relation to Jesus Christ and in relation to

THE LISTENING PARISH

all others who are in a relationship with Christ. Each of the *Christifideles* completes the presence of Jesus Christ in the world, and each completes all others of the *Christifideles* in relationship with Christ and one another.

The Whole People of God

Thus, Vatican II defines and expresses the life of the Church in dynamic, relational terms. The Church's lifeblood surges in reciprocity and complementarity among all the *Christifideles* believing, worshiping, speaking, and acting together in mission.

This principle of the Church being relational invites us to understand that the whole people of God carries out the Church's mission. The whole *Christifideles* accomplishes the Church's mission when we integrate and express the diversity and originality of our gifts and services, joining together in common participation with everyone in the Church. Indeed, continual, reciprocal interaction among all the *Christifideles* constitutes and reconstitutes us as the people of God.

The Hierarchy and Laity Together

Note: the faithful of Christ (*Christifideles* literally translated) are not only the laity, which is how the term *the faithful* has often been used. Instead, all the baptized are the *Christifideles*. *Faithful* and *laity* are not interchangeable terms. The people of God, the *Christifideles*, comprises all who share the relational dignity of baptism: the laity and the ordained.

Consequently, under the principles that the whole has priority over its parts and the end holds priority over the means, the role of the hierarchy in the Church is to serve the whole people of God for the sake of mission. The hierarchy's role is not to enforce a vertical chain of command. Instead, it aims to be the initial discerners who search for unity and consensus among the whole people of God that expresses the sense of the entire Church together. It is to build up affective and effective collegiality horizontally across the whole Church.

> In this Church, as an inverted pyramid, the top is below the base. That is why those who exercise authority are called "ministers": according to the original meaning of the word, they are the least of all.
>
> Pope Francis, 17 October 2015

A New Way of Proceeding

Accomplishing the Church's mission demands a way of proceeding that searches for ways to carry out the mission with the participation of all. It requires an ecclesial style that organically links the functions, tasks, ministries, states of life, and charisms of the whole people of God, all the *Christifideles*.

All the baptized, moving from the periphery to the center and back again, listening, discerning, and being accountable together—the pope, the bishops, and the laity—is the dynamic action constituting the Church and continually transforming it on the synodal way.

CONSIDERING SYNODALITY

Co-Responsibility & Respect

Facing the Hierarchical Structure

The Church has a many centuries history of hierarchical culture. Age-old theologies, caste structures, customs, dress codes, leadership philosophies, management practices, and organizational assumptions continue to support and sustain a robust hierarchical structure in the Church.

Honesty requires that we concede with gratitude that the hierarchical clerical culture has upheld the Church through some turbulent times.

Honesty also requires that we concede that the clerical culture remains durable in our time. That is, we would be wise to accept that the Church shall likely remain hierarchical whatever the clergy's culture.

Given these realities, how do we understand, configure, and live well together regarding the clergy-lay interrelationship in a synodal Church?

The Vatican II Way: Diversity in Unity

Baptism organically grafts all of us into the priestly, prophetic, and kingly life of Christ through the Holy Spirit in the Church. The Christifideles, the people of God, are incorporated into Jesus Christ's teaching, governing, and sanctifying ministry of communion, and we have co-responsibility for it.

All the Christifideles are commissioned to the ministry of the Word; all are co-responsible and accountable for it.

Through the sacrament of holy orders, some among the people of God are commissioned to ministerial function: serving the whole Christifideles' mission and presiding over the community in the person of Christ. The ordained serve as a symbol of communion for the Church and a symbol of the extension over time of Christ's mission to proclaim the Gospel to the world.

Within the Christifideles, among the people of God, the bishops, in college with the presiding ministry of the Bishop of Rome, oversee the Church's teaching, governing, and sanctifying mission. Presbyters (priests), in college with the bishop, serve as the bishop's co-workers. Presbyters are commissioned to preach the Gospel, preside over community life, coordinate pastoral ministry, and extend pastoral care; thus, they preside in Eucharist. Deacons serve in college as co-workers with the bishops and priests, charged particularly to preach the Gospel and to the pastoral ministry of charity; thus, deacons proclaim the Word and minister the Blood of Christ in the Eucharist.

THE LISTENING PARISH

> Among the more important duties of bishops that of preaching the Gospel has pride of place.
>
> *Lumen Gentium* 25

> …it is the first task of priests as co-workers with the bishops to preach the Gospel of God to all men [and women].
>
> *Presbyterium Ordinis* 4

Both the priesthood of all the Christifideles and the ordained ministry within the Christifideles expressed in the sacrament of holy orders, are rooted in baptism. Both are commissioned primarily to spread the Gospel. Both participate in the one priesthood of Christ.

Within this marvelous diversity of co-responsible ministries, the common priesthood of the people of God brought about through baptism is the starting point for the Church's life.

Among the people of God, hierarchical ministry is oriented toward the search for unity, not by a vertical command structure, but by the Church's nature as a complementary, respectful, and co-responsible communion of priestly, prophetic, and royal people commissioned to spread the Gospel.

The Church is Teamwork

Within these co-responsible relationships, no one is secondary, no one subordinate. The lay Christifideles are not oriented exclusively toward the world and the ordained people of God exclusively toward the Church.

> It is impossible to think of a conversion of our activity as a Church that does not include the active participation of all the members of God's People.
>
> Pope Francis August 20, 2018

All the people of God are essential for the whole of the Church's ministry. All the Christifideles are necessary for all stages of the Church's ministry because all are agents of the Church's mission to the world.

In our time, we have the wonderful opportunity to structure mechanisms and processes at all levels of the Church, beginning with the parish, so that all the Christifideles might listen, discern, decide, elaborate, and evaluate decisions together. Only a synodal style ensures that our decisions represent the consensus of the Church and remain transparently accountable to all the people of God. Only in this way of proceeding in a culture of encounter, with all participating together, listening to one another, discerning together, deciding together, planning together, ministering together, and evaluating together, can the whole Church community open to the transforming power of the Holy Spirit in accompanying one another effectively in fulfilling the Church's mission.

To word this principle differently: when all the Christifideles in common processes accept the binding nature of listening to all, discerning together, deciding by consensus, and implementing decisions together in an accountable way, the Church confidently establishes the true sense of all the faithful in communion together.

Always Looking to the Whole and to the Mission

Synodal Church life in a culture of encounter requires that all the Christifideles focus passionately on our common mission to preach the Gospel through words and acts of humble service, bearing witness in our leadership structures, life together, and outward encounter and accompaniment to our experience of the mercy of God offered us through Jesus Christ.

Synodal Church life demands that all the people of God strive to link and integrate all the Church's communal leadership structures, from the universal level to the local parish level, and create constructive interaction among them.

Synodality demands that all the Christifideles, each with his or her faith experience, existential context, personal wisdom, and ministerial commission—ordained and lay together—sit around one table of unity and accompaniment to forge together consensus about the fulfillment of the Church's mission in our particular time and place.

A synodal Church works to respect, include, and listen to the whole people of God, encountering and accompanying one another as Church. ∎

CONSIDERING SYNODALITY

Beliefs Grounding Synodality

The Necessary Foundation

Synodality is a mindset, a fundamentally spiritual attitude about our life together as Church that rests on convictions about God's will, what the Church is, the sacraments, and the Christifideles. If we embrace synodality practices, certain beliefs must ground what we do and how we do it as Church. Without them, our embrace of synodality will be weak or partial, or it will fail.

- **Renewal**: The *Lumen Gentium* model of the Church as the people of God on a **pilgrimage** toward the Father sets a model and vision of Church for our time.
- Baptism empowers the people of God as the organically **united Christifideles** in the midst of the world.
- Baptism also empowers the universal Christifideles to be **missionary disciples** of Christ.
- The **mission** of the people of God is to bring the Gospel to the whole world, excluding no one.
- **Solidarity**: All the Christifideles are responsible for nurturing the communion that is Church and fulfilling the Church's mission.
- **Option for the poor**: The Christifideles includes the poor as privileged subjects among us. The poor are not simply the economically deprived but include all those on the peripheries of society and the margins of the Church who live without full acceptance.
- The **ordained** serve the whole Christifideles as one among the people of God.
- **Women and men religious** serve the whole Christifideles through the exercise of their charism.
- The **laity** serve the Christifideles through their personal gifts, expertise, life experience, and the hard-won insight they gain through their lives of faith.
- **Participation**: By definition, the Church is a dynamic relational reality: a people building communion together as they proclaim the Word, share their gifts, and advance together on a pilgrimage toward God.
- **Discernment** builds the Church as all the baptized, with their vocations, charisms, ministries, and services, hear the Word, examine the signs of the times, and participate together in concrete space and time under the action of the Holy Spirit.
- **Dignity of the human person**: All of the Christifideles can know and express truths about the content of our faith.
- All the Christifideles are a necessary part of the whole, including a wonderful **diversity** of charisms, gifts, services, and ministries, completing the whole.
- **Communion**: To listen to God, we must listen to the whole Christifideles so that we might, together, through actions, words, and gestures, hear, distinguish, and interpret the many voices of our age.
  - Synodality is a **communal** form of living and interacting in a culture of encounter and sharing. Church is not an individual experience; we are Church only if we are interrelated.
- What affects all should be discussed and approved by all.
- The aim of our listening, discussing, discern-

THE LISTENING PARISH

ing, deciding, and implementing decisions together is to achieve **consensus** about how we as the people of God fulfill our baptismal communion and mission.

* *Sensus fidelium*: Consensus is neither a mere organizational matter nor a simple redistribution of position and power. The achieving of consensus brings the Church to new birth.

* The first and last question of our listening and discerning processes, indeed all our complex interactions, is always: **what does God wants of us?**

* Listening requires the personal **involvement of the ordained** as one of the Christifideles: learning from other participants, engaging in dialogue, respecting different points of view, risking change, and, in the process, becoming an integral part of the consensus achieved.

* **When points of view oppose one another**, the ordained need to listen even more closely because the responsibility to listen and express oneself flows from the gifts the Holy Spirit pours forth on all the baptized.

* **Subsidiarity**: Only if all the Christifideles engage in expressing themselves, listen to one another, discern together, consult relevant persons, and decide together can the making and implementing of decisions have full and final authority.

* The Church is credible only if it is itself evangelized by **constant renewal and conversion**.

CONSIDERING SYNODALITY

What Synodality is Not

Certain themes in United States culture and that of many Western democracies inform many of our people's understanding of governance and coming to decisions as we gather around a leadership table. These democratic themes arise from national history and the wide affirmation we give, generation after generation, to our governmental structures.

These themes, however, can create conflict for many who share in parish leadership and life because the Church's grounding, structure, and priorities differ markedly from those of the nation. While synodality has certain elements we might off-handedly consider democratic, a synodal way of proceeding as Church differs from what many Western cultures understand as democracy. Consequently, it is necessary to clarify what the synodal way is not.

Communion, Not Representation

The cry at the time of the U. S. Boston Tea Party was "No taxation without representation!" Ever since, American constitutional tradition seeks representation for the people's opinion on every issue of concern to the commonweal.

The democratic notion of representation includes the understanding that a person comes forward in group leadership to stand up for a constituency so its voice can be heard. This notion presumes a certain "us" and "them" in gathering for group decision-making.

While representation might need to be broadly considered in a parish's council or a parish assembly, synodality invites us to search for means and methods for the direct participation of all. That may include extended forms of consultation of those on the edges of parish life, including collating their discussion results or direct participation in assembly events. Therefore, our task over the coming years is to seek communication forms and meeting structures that include everyone in listening, discerning, decision-making, implementing, and evaluating. On the synodal way, no one may be excluded.

Though we have much work to do as a Church and much to learn about as we seek to shape a thoroughly synodal way of proceeding, our aim is ever-fuller communion, not simply registering representation.

Participation, Not Checks and Balances

The notion of checks and balances in a democracy's governance leaves a people feeling secure in the interplay of our governmental institutions. However, checks and balances presume polarity—sometimes cooperative, sometimes adversarial—within our national life and among its various structures.

In a synodal Church, the whole Christifideles gathers to listen to one another, discern direction, make decisions, implement action, and evaluate forward movement to spread Jesus Christ's Gospel of mercy and caring for the world.

Transparency and accountability among the whole Christifideles are high values that need to be kept solidly in place, resting as they do in the whole people of God moving forward together in unity as one body.

A synodal way of proceeding is not about checks and balances. Instead, it is about the whole Christifideles participating together in shaping our Gospel mission and growing in unity simultaneously.

Discernment Toward Consensus, Not Majority Rule Legislation

Our democratic notion of the decision-making

process in governance is that legislators exchange wide points of view among as many as possible and then the majority comes to an agreement through a majority vote on the best course for the most. Decision-making processes in a democracy presume majority rule and some horse-trading to get to it. The result of that process is law.

In a synodal way of proceeding, the majority's perspective is an important datum in decision-making but is neither the whole story nor the aim of the process.

A synodal Church aims to build the faithful's consensus toward what God wants. This process is subject to internal and external verification over time, sometimes a long time. Synodality engages the whole Church in listening to one another and the movement of the Holy Spirit among us so we might proceed together in unity in our Gospel mission, even changing our way of seeing and doing things for its sake.

A synodal way of proceeding, though it might include making law at times, is not an essentially legislative process.

Moreover, the synodal way is never about majority rule. Synodal practice is about building consensus.

Being Clear About the Differences

As our various Church communities learn about the above differences between ecclesial and democratic leadership group assumptions, that will help ease both fears and difficulties in implementing synodal practices across the Church.

By Way of Example

Evelyn was widely experienced in city politics, twice running for office. She sought election to the parish's pastoral council. Knowing her experience well, Fr. John, the pastor, asked Evelyn if she would mind coming in for a conversation about council leadership. She agreed.

When they met, Fr. John explained council leadership expectations, underlining for Evelyn the differences between common democratic presuppositions and ecclesial ones. The ensuing conversation was comfortable and clarifying.

Evelyn finally concluded, "You know, Father, that doesn't fit me at all. I don't think serving on the pastoral council is a good idea for me."

Their conversation deepened Evelyn's and Fr. John's mutual understanding and shared concerns about the parish. Fr. John grew in admiration of Evelyn's self-awareness, realism, and honesty even as Evelyn's reconsideration alleviated confusion about the manner of decision-making policy on the pastoral council.

CONSIDERING SYNODALITY

Thought-Provoking Images

To help convey a picture of what synodality ought to look like in the parish, the two following images intend to offer food for thought. The first draws a whole parish picture. The second illustrates synodality from the angle of the parish leadership group.

The Symbol of the Chair

The focal symbol of the bishop's authority in a diocese is the cathedra, the chair in his see city from which he presides at Eucharist. The cathedra holds such symbolic weight that one church in every diocese is built to house it: the cathedral, the church of the chair.

When the bishop presides from the cathedra surrounded by the priests, deacons, religious, and laity of the diocese, the whole Christifideles is symbolically present—the local and the universal Church—in its organic unity as the one people of God, the one Body of Christ.

The presider's chair in the parish church stands as a symbol of the cathedra and participates in its reality. That is, the parish presider's chair is the bishop's chair, a symbol of the universal, organic unity of the Church, in the parish church. The presider's chair is entrusted to the pastor as the bishop's co-worker, who is installed in the bishop's chair in the parish assembly to proclaim the Gospel, preside in sacrament, especially the Eucharist, and direct the pastoral care of the parish community.

THE CHAIR WITHIN THE ASSEMBLY

Kenneth Untener was Bishop of the Diocese of Saginaw, Michigan, from 1980 to 2004. To walk into the Cathedral of the Assumption during Bishop Untener's tenure was to be startled and challenged by its physical arrangement. No cathedra sat in the sanctuary facing the assembly, its typical placement in most cathedrals worldwide. Instead, in Bishop Untener's cathedral the cathedra sat within the assembly facing forward toward the ambo and altar.

This cathedra placement proclaimed that Bishop Untener saw himself as one among the people of God, commissioned to a particular leadership role for the Saginaw Church, and conspicuously so. Still, like all the Christifideles, the bishop was subject to the Word of God and its transforming power and co-responsible with all the Christifideles for proclaiming that Word. Bishop Untener only faced the assembly when preaching within the Liturgy of the Word or presiding within the Liturgy of the Eucharist.

The image of the parish presider's chair sitting within the assembly, among all the people of God, offers a provocative picture of who we are as Church—lay and ordained together: what we baptized share in common, how our service differs, and the humility to which we are called in one another's presence as listeners, decision-makers, implementers, and evaluators of our common mission to proclaim the Gospel of mercy to the world.

The Symbol of the Table

Eucharist is the source and summit of our life as a faith community. Within the Liturgy of the Word, we break open the Scriptures at the table of God's Word, the ambo. Within the Liturgy of the Eucharist, we eat and drink the Body and Blood of the Risen Lord at the altar table.

Our two-table Eucharistic event opens us to the breath of the Holy Spirit's life and the fire of the Spirit's power within and among us as a people. What we do around the table of the Word and the table of the Eucharist feeds us as a people of faith, drawing us further, deeper, and ever more meaningfully and vulnerably into communion with God and one another. The ambo and altar, therefore, are noble pieces of furniture located prominently in the church, at the parish's heart. They are tall tables, 39 inches tall, elegantly fashioned for august purpose.

But there is a third table where we are fed in parish life: the parish meeting table.

THE LOW, ROUND PARISH MEETING TABLE

The parish meeting table serves the purposes of gracious hospitality and reflective listening and dialogue. Vital to parish life and a symbol of who we are, the pastoral leadership table sits humbly alongside the table of the Word and the table of the Eucharist as a place where heaven and earth meet in parish life.

The parish meeting table is most properly round because pastoral meetings aim to build consensus, common mind, heart, and purpose among the baptized, diverse equals who share a common mission and co-responsibility for it. This purpose requires deep listening and a free flow of ideas among the Christifideles—lay and ordained together. It requires power-sharing, growth in transparency, accountability, and trust within the Church community and beyond it.

The parish meeting table is ideally low, 17 inches, because drawing together in unity requires vulnerability. The first question that governs pastoral discernment—what does God want of us?—calls all the people of God who gather around it to open to the divine life within them, among them, and within the whole parish community, especially those on the peripheries. The need to listen, share forthrightly, risk self-knowledge, decide, plan, implement, and evaluate together to common purpose demands a low table. Often, this engagement includes conflicting views, eliciting a deep vulnerability in listening and dialogue and calling participants to profound mutual respect.

Considering Physical Space

Physical space creates an atmosphere that proclaims to all who share in it their identity and purpose. A distant throne speaks of power and otherness. Sitting together around a shared focus proclaims commonality. A high table covered with papers and pencils, with people leaning back away from it or leaning forward with arms crossed, especially under glaring fluorescent light, speaks of work or a psychological joust. A low table in soft light—plates of cookies, coffee mugs, milk glasses, and napkins in the center—invites people to graciousness, conveys warm regard, and implicitly respects the assembled as honored persons whose opinions are highly valued.

For Your Consideration

Perhaps these images can help us think through who we are and what it might take for us as the people of God to truly listen to and accept one another as Christifideles with understanding and a willingness even to sacrifice for our common mission.

THE SYNODAL PATH FOR THE PARISH

THE SYNODAL PATH FOR THE PARISH
Probing Practices Questions

The Call and the Practice in the Parish

Practical responses to the call to become a listening and discerning Church require that we enter into the process of becoming ever more fully the Christifideles, the people of God. This call has universal and local dimensions.

Pope Francis has made clear:

* Papal primacy and episcopal collegiality require reform.

* Ordained ministry needs reconfiguration to address the real issues surrounding the exercise of power and authority.

* Primacy, collegiality, and ordained ministry must be re-imagined in the context of the Vatican II vision of the people of God.

* All the above must be reconsidered and reshaped in the light of the spiritual discernment framework offered by synodality.

Pope Francis lays before us an ambitious, daunting project that needs to incubate and grow into the fullness of life in the Holy Spirit on the universal, continental, national, regional, diocesan, and parish levels.

This process requires experimentation. Entering it demands creativity and patience. We have yet to apply, or even discover, many of the tools we need to achieve the vision held up before us. Sustaining the process for the long haul will demand of the Church profoundly faith-filled trust in what the Holy Spirit is saying to the churches.

The Parish: Seedbed for Synodality

As we, the people of God, move forward with enlarging the space in our tent, entrusting ourselves to the Holy Spirit as listeners and discerners, many questions surface, especially about parish life. Why? The process we are entering needs to be incubated with local processes and practices

THE LISTENING PARISH

which the larger Church will later express.

Consequently, it is wise for us to focus our questions and begin to address them, mindful that more will arise:

* What are the relationship structures between the diocese and the parish?
* What concerns might invite us to consider new relationship structures?
* What is the pastor's/priest's role in the parish?
* How might the pastor's/priest's role be best exercised? What are the options?
* What is the place of the pastoral council in the parish?
* What is the pastoral council's relationship to planning?
* What is the place of the finance council in the parish?
* What is the finance council's relationship to planning?
* What is the pastor's/priest's place within each council?
* What are the councils' relationships with each other?
* What are the councils' relationships with the whole parish?
* How does parish size impact the shape of its discernment leadership?
* How are the whole parish's concerns gathered?
* How are larger Church issues discussed in the parish?
* How are conflicts resolved?
* How is the advice and participation of the whole parish engaged in leadership?
* What does accountability look like? Who is accountable for what? To whom?
* What is the parish's organizational chart?
* Where do parish staff members most properly fit?
* How do we understand different levels of responsibility among staff?
* What are the concerns about staff hiring, supervision, and termination we need to be concerned about?
* How are those on the peripheries engaged in discernment leadership?
* Where are the peripheries?
* What are cultural pitfalls that everyone in the parish needs to understand?
* How is discernment/decision-making implemented in a parish's leadership groups?
* How is discernment/decision-making implemented in the parish as a whole?
* What ought a council meeting look and feel like?
* How are council members selected?
* What are the eligibility requirements for council leadership?
* What is the place of confidentiality in discernment and decision-?
* When is the bishop engaged in parish matters?
* How does the parish handle conflict?

Answering these Questions

Reflecting on these questions helps pastoral leadership, in reciprocal listening and dialogue, assess the parish's place on the road. Discerning what practices might be necessary to improve the synodal journey stirs a parish to forward movement. Taking further steps on the synodal path opens our community to becoming an ever more authentically listening and discerning Church: Christifideles, the people of God on mission to the world. ∎

THE SYNODAL PATH FOR THE PARISH

Parish Practices for the Journey

The Sober Truth

Synodal practice aims for the ongoing transformation of the parish community and the Church. While it has been integral to the life of the Church since at least 50 A.D. (see Acts of the Apostles, Chapter 15), synodality's expression has been narrowed across the centuries.

Journeying toward the synodal way, consequently, takes patience, time, and effort. It requires experimentation with methods and structures for communication—outreach, listening, dialogue, decision-making, implementing decisions, and evaluating—that have yet to be used in the Church—or perhaps even invented.

Moreover, our experience of synodality is hampered. Elements of Church law, worship, and custom hinder synodality's full development. Some hierarchy and clergy drag their feet implementing it or stand against it. Synodal processes and their effectiveness vary from one nation and culture to another. Participation in the universal Church process, though enthusiastic, has yet to meet the high standards of engagement, numbers, and effectiveness that a full synodal embrace demands.

Though filled with hope, our expectations require flexible creativity, informed patience, and sober engagement with reality.

Implementing Synodality Practices in the Parish

Consequently, our Church situation suggests that a parish should carefully consider how to proceed on the synodal way.

Each parish has a distinct diocesan context and geography, a unique history, culture, and personality. Each community progresses through life phases of building, thriving in stride, then stagnating, only to move into building again. We need to analyze and understand these contexts.

Nonetheless, the journey to a synodal Church begins by implementing certain concrete synodality practices in the parish.

The practices below suggest themselves for fashioning a parish toward the synodal journey. Without them, synodal style cannot be implemented. Without all of them, the journey would be hobbled and incomplete. Any parish community would do well to consider these practices, discern the parish's relative position, and begin or continue the way in accord with them.

Win the Pastor's Support

How the parish's pastoral leader exercises his or her ministry is crucial to synodal practice. The parish needs the pastoral leader's firm support and participation.

The diocesan bishop's position also needs to be understood. He may be passive or offer a parish resources. Knowing the bishop's perspective and support level helps.

Nurture Well-Working Councils

As its local bishop, Pope Francis began the synodal path in the Diocese of Rome by mandating pastoral councils in all parishes. Accountable to the pastor, the parish assembly, and the bishop, the pastoral council's role in shaping ministry and co-responsibility in the parish is integral to the synodal way.

A well-functioning finance council is also crucial. Accountable stewardship of parish resources is critical to building trust. Lack of financial, legal, personnel, and property transparency and accountability blocks trust.

Council effectiveness depends on the pastor's and councils' embracing ongoing planning, publicly committing to the broad participation of parishioners and outside experts, and moving out to the peripheries.

Implement Discernment Decision-Making

The practice of discernment decision-making across all leadership groups opens the community to the transforming gifts and power of the Holy Spirit. Reciprocal listening and dialogue aim toward consensus. Even conflict can yield to new avenues of pastoral response. The pastor's participation as one-among-many is integral to discernment's success.

Shape a Collegial Parish Staff

The pastoral leader and staff need to embrace a collegial style of ministry. Pastoral staff members need to embrace a collegial style of ministering with parishioners. Collegial exercise of pastoral leadership serves as a formation seedbed for ministry participation and synodality practice across the parish.

Follow Just Employment Practices

Justice, the right ordering of relationships for building up the common good of the parish and beyond, stands out as a fundamental Gospel call. Credibility on the synodal way for leadership and parishioners rests on pastoral leadership's being just in all it does, including employment practices.

Engage the Parish Assembly

Pastoral leadership needs to shape an effective communication program within the parish. Clear, careful, reciprocal, and constant communication can be a parish bugaboo. Effective communication among leadership groups and with the whole parish is a necessarily flexible, ongoing, and ever-challenging experiment in a parish.

Building effective listening, dialogue, and accountability structures and methods includes establishing regular parish assembly engagement. Developing a parish-wide commitment to listening to all, with everyone participating co-responsibly in parish decision-making, requires time and ever-shifting experimentation with methods.

All These Practices...

...equip a parish for the synodal way.

CHURCH STRUCTURE

CHURCH STRUCTURE

The Diocese

Implementing synodality practices holds enormous implications for the expectations surrounding parish governance. Consequently, understanding synodality practice in a parish requires understanding the relationships with entities and persons within and outside the parish. These relationships rest on foundational theological principles and have legal structures in Church and civil law that need to be understood.

Universal Church Structure

The Roman Catholic Church is "one Body" composed of two dispensations, two systems of order: West and East. Each dispensation is regulated by its own rules, called canon law. The Western Dispensation comprises seven ritual communities; the Eastern includes 23. Each of these 30 communities is called a *rite*, which refers to how the sacraments are celebrated in related but distinct cultural and historical traditions.

By far, the largest of the ritual families in the universal constellation that is the Roman Catholic Church is the Latin Rite of the Western Dispensation.

The Diocese

Within all the rites—East and West—a particular church is called a *diocese*. The term, which originated in ancient Roman imperial law, refers to a defined territory and the people within it presided over by a bishop.

Theologically, a diocese is neither a branch of the Universal Church nor a division of it. Rather, the diocese is the fundamental unit that constitutes the Church. It embodies in a particular territory, with a particular community, the whole Catholic Church as an organic unity.[1]

> A diocese is a portion of the people of God which is entrusted for pastoral care to a bishop with the cooperation of the presbyterate so that, adhering to its pastor and gathered by him in the Holy Spirit through the gospel and the Eucharist, it constitutes a particular church in which the one, holy, catholic, and apostolic Church of Christ is truly present and operative.
>
> Canon 369

In theology and law, the diocese—not the parish and not the individual Catholic—stands as the most fundamental realization of the Church in space and time. The bishop is placed at its center as the symbol of continuity and universality.

The Bishop

As the chief shepherd of a diocese, the bishop is the visible source and foundation of unity for the diocese.[2] As the holder of a pastoral office charged to protect the unity of both the universal Church and the diocese, the bishop is bound to promote the common discipline of the Church.

> Through the Holy Spirit who has been given to them, bishops are the successors of the apostles by divine institution; they are constituted pastors within the Church so that they are teachers of doctrine, priests of sacred worship, and ministers of governance.
>
> Canon 375

The bishop exercises legislative, executive, and judicial power within the diocese subject to the norms of canon law (can. 391, 392).

---

1 See the Vatican II *Decree on the Pastoral Office of Bishops in the Church*, #22.
2 See the Vatican II *Dogmatic Constitution on the Church*, #23, and *Decree on Bishops*, #11.

The Chairs as Symbols of Unity

A focal symbol of the bishop's authority in a diocese is the cathedra, the chair he presides from in worship. The cathedra holds such weight as a symbol that a church is built to house it: the cathedral, the church of the chair. The local cathedra also serves as a symbol of universal communion with the Bishop of Rome.

The far eastern altar in St. Peter's is dominated by a huge bronze chair encasing a smaller chair, which tradition holds was used by St. Peter. The papal ministry is officially called "The Holy See," a quaint English term meaning "The Holy Chair." Every February 22, Catholics celebrate a feast called The Chair of Peter.

The presider's chair in the parish church stands as a symbol of the cathedra and participates in its two-fold symbolic reality. The presider's chair in the parish assembly is the bishop's chair in the church and a symbol of his authority and his unity with the Bishop of Rome. The presider's chair is entrusted to the pastor as a co-worker with the bishop—in his communion with the Bishop of Rome and the universal college of bishops—charged with the pastoral care of a parish community.

The Diocese in U.S. Civil Law

The diocese also has a civil law structure in order to own property, regulate finances, and transact business legally in the United States. In the U.S., all dioceses are legal corporations recognized by the state. This corporate structure takes one of two forms.

One is the "corporation sole" diocese, in which all the parishes and institutions of the diocese are part of the integral whole that is a single legal corporation.

In the other, each institution in the diocese is established as a separate corporation. In this model, each corporation—the diocese itself is often designated as the central corporation—is regulated by its own corporate board. The board usually includes the bishop as chair, diocesan officials, and, in the case of a parish, the pastor, and local parishioners.

The Civil Law Implications

The corporate status of the parish, and the pastor's critical responsibilities as a fiduciary render the pastor not only responsible to the bishop but also legally and inalienably responsible in civil law for all matters of

❋ law,

❋ personnel,

❋ property,

❋ and finances.

CHURCH STRUCTURE

Parish Civil Law Status

The Parish

In Church law, a parish is a certain community of the Christian faithful stably constituted in a diocese. As a rule, a parish is geographical; it includes all the Christian faithful of a certain territory (can. 518).

Note that a parish can also be national. In the U.S., national parishes were established in the late 19th and early 20th centuries in large cities for particular ethnic communities. This bridge structure for the parish was done to facilitate the group's being more comfortably enculturated and educated for integration into U.S. society.

The legal status of the community as a parish established within a diocese remains essentially the same whether the parish's leader is a diocesan priest, from a religious order, a deacon, or a layperson.

For all parishes, a synodal way of proceeding must consider a parish's civil law structure and relationships carefully.

Corporation Sole Diocese

While the pastor or parish leader serves no official corporate function in a corporation sole diocese—the bishop is the chairman of the corporation and may be, in himself, the corporate board—the pastor's service of good order may be considered roughly analogous to that of a CEO serving on the corporation's behalf.

The purposes of the corporation sole are:

* to support Gospel ministry by assisting the bishop in administering the diocese's temporal affairs,

* to hold property for the use and benefit of and in trust for the diocese and the respective Catholic entities located within the geographical boundaries of the diocese,

* to hold property to honor restrictions placed on its use by donors or others,

* to have perpetual succession and existence as afforded to a corporation under state law.

Corporation Sole and Parish

The corporation sole has the legal authority to transact business and set guidelines for the pastor's and parish's acts. The following is but one example of a diocesan corporation sole's guidelines:

* The pastor may act alone in financial and property transactions of less than $1,000.

* For transactions between $1,000 and $5,000, the pastor must seek the counsel of the parish pastoral and finance councils before taking action.

* For transactions between $5,000 and $10,000, before he may act, the pastor must seek the counsel of the parish pastoral and finance councils and submit a request to the bishop, who approves or disapproves.

* For transactions above $10,000, the pastor must seek the counsel of the pastoral and finance councils, submit a request to the bishop, and submit a request to the diocesan finance council, which acts as a consultative body to the bishop by making formal recommendations for his consideration and decision.

Disregarding these guidelines, especially in larger matters, usually brings about great stress in relationship with the bishop and can even lead to disciplinary measures, including the stoppage of planned projects. Flouting the rules can also lead to pastor replacement.

Multi-Corporation Dioceses

Many dioceses of the U.S. comprise a cluster of corporations. Each unit within the diocese, as well as the diocesan office itself, forms a legal corporation legally bound to the bishop.

To form a corporate board within this structure, the bishop associates himself with, for instance, the vicar general, the pastor (in the case of a parish), and two designated parishioners, who are called trustees and function as corporate secretary and treasurer. This group serves as the legal corporation. As both the board and the corporation, these five officers together have the authority to transact corporate business and are legally required to do so.

Though the bishop chairs the corporate board, the pastor serves as CEO of the parish. The corporate board, however, remains a fundamental collegial pastoral leadership context for a parish and pastor.

This corporate structure also means that the diocese remains in control of a parish. The bishop's office, therefore, sets guidelines for the expenditure of funds and disposition of property. Though guidelines differ among dioceses, a parish typically requires corporate board permission to transact business in the following circumstances:

* The sale, purchase, mortgage, and receiving of gifts of real estate;
* the granting of easements;
* lease or rental agreements;
* stock transfers or sales;
* capital improvements over $15,000;
* new construction;
* service contracts;
* the borrowing of money;
* and litigation.

In this model, too, following the rules is always the wise course.

When Following the Rules Goes Awry

Fr. Justin inherited a parish with a $2 million debt. In the hope of priming the pump to win parish commitment to paying down the debt, he decided to do make $60,000 sacrament chapel improvement to help set a vision for the parish.

Fr. Justin solicited private donations to fund the project. He dragged his feet, however, regarding permissions, failing to gain from the start parish leadership, parish community, and diocesan committee support for the project and his plans.

The bishop happened to get wind of the project. Unaware of Fr. Justin's methodology and ill-disposed to considering it, the bishop—by letter—told him to shut the project down, give the money back, and do a capital campaign to retire the debt.

A Special Consideration: Corporate Trustees

A parish corporation raises a special concern around parish governance. How does a parish meld the parish's corporate trustees into the pastoral leadership structure?

Some parishes hold the trustees apart from governance structures either as personal counselors to the pastor as he wishes or as free-floating parishioners without involvement beyond their corporate duties.

In other parishes, one trustee, the secretary of the corporation, serves as a pastoral council member. The other trustee, the corporate treasurer, serves on the finance council. This power distribution integrates the corporation into the advisory structure of the parish and keeps the trustees, and therefore, with the pastor, the corporate board majority, closely informed about the parish's state and plans. It also allows the trustees to make ongoing public contributions to the parish's forward movement.

Dissociation of the trustees from a leadership role risks various forms of stress for a parish: breakdown of basic information-sharing, clergy gang-up on the trustees in formal corporate actions, making light of the corporation's place in governance, undercutting the rightful place of parishioner representation on the corporate board, and the build-up of trustee resentment, which can lead them to make end runs to the bishop and even publicly oppose a pastor.

The form of trustee association with parish pastoral leadership warrants careful reflection and wise structuring.

CHURCH STRUCTURE

Parish and Leadership Variation

A U.S. Parish Snapshot

In 2021, the United States had over 16,579 Catholic parishes serving 66.8 million registered Catholic adults (over 71 million when people self-reported). Over 13,200 of these parishes had a resident priest pastor. The average size of the U.S. Catholic parish was 1,168 households.

Around 3,300 parishes were family parishes (200 or fewer registered households) or community parishes (201-549 households). These parishes had varied pastoral leadership arrangements. The remaining 10,000 parishes in the U.S. were mega-parishes (over 1200 households) and corporate parishes (550-1200 households in multiple settings).

Family and Community Parishes

Family and community parishes often have four staff members: pastor, secretary, part-time religious formation person, and a part-time bookkeeper.

Stereotypically, the secretary holds enormous power in this parish situation simply because she is full-time in the parish office while no one else is.

These parish situations require communication flexibility. Ought there be a formal group staff meeting? Who participates? Is communication adequate without it?

Mutually agreeable consistency assures relative comfort, but each situation requires a sensitive approach based on personalities and parish needs.

The Mega-Parish

The largest Catholic parish in the U.S. had 10,500 registered households in 2021. This size community of communities brings with it unique concerns.

First, the expectation that the pastor will have a personal relationship with a large portion of the parish is unreasonable, especially when only 24% of Catholics attend Mass on a given weekend.

The larger mega-parish often has several staff members in a Gospel ministry area: for example, in the area of religious education, a pastoral associate for family religious formation, one for sacramental formation, one for adult formation, and one for youth ministry. These, in turn, have their own support staff.

Staff members entrusted with ministry service in collegial relationship with and accountable to a pastoral associate are often a cross between pastoral and administrative staff.

In general, staff relationships in a single or blended area of Gospel ministry should be treated like the relationship between pastor and pastoral staff, with the pastoral associate functioning with

his or her staff like the pastor does with the pastoral staff.

The pastor and pastoral associates must decide who supervises and reports to whom, who comes to what meetings, and what patterns of communication work to cohere the parish's ministry in general and in given situations.

While consistent practices assure comfort for all, the mega-parish pastoral team has much juggling to do to maintain balance.

Corporate Parishes

Clustered parishes present a touchy challenge because they are often a mix of small and large communities, some sites closer and others farther apart, that remain sensitive to their differences, prerogatives, and favoritism. Clustered situations can be highly complex.

For such a circumstance—country or city—staff structure options are essentially three: a centralized, a blended, or an extension model.

Centralized staffing assumes that one site, the largest or most centrally located, will function like a "cathedral" for the cluster. This model suggests a single set of Gospel ministry pastoral associates who oversee ministry areas at all sites. Administrative staff members are hired to assist depending on parish and site resources. This model relies on the cluster's single pastoral council and finance council.

The **blended staffing** model assumes the distinct identity of each site and strives to honor that identity while simultaneously seeking to shape a coherent Gospel ministry across the cluster. This model would establish some full-time and part-time site-connected pastoral associates who minister with the pastor, the people at each site, and other staff members hired to help, depending on the cluster's, or a site's resources. The site-connected pastoral associates coordinate ministry at each location.

The **extension staffing** model assumes distinct site identity while making little effort to cohere the disparate communities. This model usually serves small parish sites well. This loose, often transitional model blesses whatever is at each site and largely relies on volunteer ministers. This model might have only a pastor and secretary full-time, with a part-time religious education coordinator and a part-time bookkeeper.

The blended and extension models may rely on separate pastoral and finance councils or blended councils, depending on site proximity, population, finances, site personalities, culture, and need.

Each model, highly dependent on local circumstances, has strengths and weaknesses. The factual situation of clusters can be even less tidy than the models. Many clusters evolve from one model to the other, or shift back and forth, because of staff and resource changes.

The Main Point

A well-informed ministry team, with alert parish support, remains critical for the parish. Parish leadership needs to understand the dynamics of its community, establish healthy and practically working listening and dialogue structures, and minister collegially if pastoral leadership is to build trust and keep it in a parish. ∎

THE PASTOR

THE PASTOR

The Parish and the Pastor

The Parish

A parish is a certain community of the Christian faithful stably constituted in a diocese. Established by the bishop, most parishes are geographically based.

> As a general rule a parish is to be territorial, that is it embraces all the Christian faithful within a certain territory; whenever it is judged useful, however, personal parishes are to be established based upon rite, language, the nationality of the Christian faithful within some territory or even upon some other determining factor. (canon 518)

Note! A geographical parish includes not simply parish members, nor only Catholics, but ALL Christian faithful within its boundaries. The parish's territory, therefore, in a primary way, shapes a parish's pastoral ministry. The needs of ALL the Christian faithful within the territory set the agenda for a parish's mission on the synodal way.

Since the 19th century in the U.S., bishops have established national parishes to serve all Christian faithful of a particular nationality or race within a specified locale.

In addition, it is crucial to note that the personal preoccupations, concerns, status, and commitments of all the people of God within a parish vastly expand the agenda of its mission.

> The parish is the presence of the Church in a given territory, an environment for hearing God's Word, for growth in the Christian life, for dialogue, proclamation, charitable outreach, worship, and celebration... a community of communities.
>
> Pope Francis, *Joy of the Gospel* 28

The Pastor

The pastoral care of a parish is entrusted to a pastor (a.k.a. parish priest) as its proper shepherd (can. 515). The pastor exercises this pastoral care under diocesan bishop's authority as a co-worker. The pastor fulfills his shepherding ministry with the cooperation of other presbyters and deacons and with the assistance of lay members of the Christian faithful (canon 519).

The Pastor's Role

Under Church law, the pastor is obliged:

* to announce the Word of God through preaching and catechesis,
* to promote the Gospel by just and charitable works,
* to oversee the education of children and evangelize,
* to ensure that the Eucharist is the center of the parish assembly of the faithful,
* to see to it that the sacraments are devoutly celebrated,
* to stimulate family prayer,
* to stimulate knowing and active participation in the sacred liturgy,
* to represent the parish in all legal affairs,
* and to oversee the parish's goods.

Church law further specifies that the pastor must strive:

* to come to know the faithful,
* to share life with the faithful,
* to acknowledge the proper role of the lay faithful in the church's mission,
* and to promote that proper role (canon 529).

From a practical point of view, in governance, the pastor's role is

* to enable, oversee, and monitor all parish Gospel ministry service;
* to strive to build consensus among the people on the parish's vision;
* to equip pastoral leaders for their ministry;
* and to ensure that pastoral leaders, paid and volunteer, are set free to do their ministry.

The Pastor's Inalienable Responsibilities

A pastor must legally consult with his pastoral and finance councils about specified matters. A wise pastor discusses matters of parish life with the parish staff and sometimes the whole parish assembly.

Nonetheless, the pastor holds certain inalienable responsibilities for the parish community. These are the matters of

* faith,
* morals,
* finances,
* property,
* law,
* and personnel.

Whatever a particular community's consultation and participation structures, the bishop and the corporation will hold only the pastor accountable for these six areas of a parish's life.

Synodal Practice and the Pastor

The synodal way is an essentially spiritual process that begins with listening, moves to discernment, then flows into decision-making, implementation, and continuing evaluation of Gospel ministry. Evaluation, itself a form of listening, begins the process again. Thus, synodal practices are a circular and ongoing transformational way of being Church.

Commitment to the synodal path demands the pastor's spiritual attitude of conversion and transformation as a way of life for himself and the parish community.

How the pastor understands his ministry and belonging within the parish community, and how he lives that understanding out, also remains critical to the synodal way. If he sees himself as one among many and participates in parish discernment decision-making as an equal, synodal practice will rest on a firm foundation in the parish.

For creating a culture of encounter and accompaniment, synodal practice depends significantly on a pastor's relational skills with the bishop, diocesan officials, parishioners, parish staff, and the poor as brothers, friends, collaborators, and cooperators in the parish's shepherding ministry and the fulfillment of its mission.

A Synodal Style Example

Fr. John inherited three city neighborhood parishes that had bumped along for 20 years in a cooperative relationship. He worked with the councils—four of them, one for each and one for the whole—to help the parishioners see that three church sites within a mile and a half of one another were untenable long-range. Eventually, the councils agreed to move toward merging the parishes.

The pastor and councils together established processes for winning diocesan approval, combining funds, coalescing staff, selecting a new parish name, the ritual closing of three sites, selling two sites, money allocation, extensive renovation of one site, the permanent placing of artifacts from all three churches, and wide dialogical communication with the whole parish throughout it all.

The brilliant touch in the process was a "question box" in which parishioners, identified or anonymous, could submit their concerns. The pastor promised to publish the submissions in the bulletin unedited, along with his answers. Mean-spirited questions accompanied by balanced, clear answers shaped by the pastor and councils garnered enormous sympathy for parish leadership and broad commitment to the merger.

The coming together took seven years to complete. The patient, highly participative process gradually won over the vast bulk of parishioners to what is one of the most unenviable tasks of contemporary parish life: dissolving multiple communities into a single happy one.

THE PASTOR
What Pastoring Requires

Skillful in Groups

In all parish settings, a pastor's ministry focuses on the whole parish assembly and the groups with it.

The synodal way demands that a pastor have significant relational and communication skills. The pastor needs to have these and, where the pastor's skills are weak, to have the wisdom and skill to authorize and encourage colleagues and parishioners who have such skills to use them on the parish's behalf. The skilled pastor participates fully in the reciprocal listening and dialogue within and among parish groups and remains firmly committed to the group processes.

A parish implementing synodal practices is best served by a pastor maestro, not a lone ranger.

The Pastor as Maestro

A maestro reveres the orchestra and strives to bring about harmonious sound from the whole of it. A maestro understands the aptitudes, strengths, and weaknesses of each of the instruments, their players, and each of the orchestra's sections.

The capable maestro has a subtle understanding of the music, too: the composer's intent, the movements within the music, and its performance history.

A maestro also knows what he or she aims to achieve with the conducting, mindful that the fullness of grace comes about only in the quality and coherence of the conductor's and orchestra's joint, capable musical execution.

For a highly skilled maestro, the orchestra's harmonious sound is more than simply the sum of its instrumental parts. Great orchestral performance is transcendent, glorious, and something new.

If a pastor has a maestro's mindset, the whole parish community always stands as the pastor's focus.

A maestro pastor learns the parish's census, geography, history, and social context. The pastor learns the community's aptitudes, strengths, weaknesses, and possibilities.

Reciprocal listening and dialogue dominate the maestro pastor's time and engagement.

The evolving of the whole together and the movements within the parish's constituent groups remain the pastor's ever-juggling focus.

If the pastoring ministry remains intentionally structured to be exercised within and among the parish's groups, then parish staff and groups feel affirmed, respected, and supported; volunteers feel blessed and encouraged; consensus builds around a shared vision; and pastoral leaders and parishioners across the community, in often surprising ways, offer amazing time and creative energy in service of the parish community and the mission.

> It terrifies me to think that I could take more pleasure in the honor attached to my office, which is where its danger lies, than in your salvation, which ought to be its fruit. This is why being set above you fills me with alarm, whereas being with you gives me comfort. Danger lies in the first; salvation in the second.
>
> St. Augustine, Sermon 340

The Lone Ranger Pastor

Fr. Archie is retiring from 13 years of pastoring St. Paul's, a large urban parish. A pious and kindly people person with a servant's heart and a good preacher, the parishioners remained taken by Fr. Archie's apparent holiness and charm. They liked him.

When asked, Fr. Archie's vision for the St. Paul's was "that the name of Jesus be known and loved." Unsure about how to translate that vision into practical terms, however, Fr. Archie consistently became defensive when pressed for details. Consequently, Fr. Archie held his cards close to his chest.

When inevitable bumps in the road showed themselves, staff and parishioners were treated to Fr. Archie's repeated refrain, "Remember, I am the pastor!" Feeling put off as a result, staff tended to jockey for favor by bending to what they guessed to be Fr. Archie's wishes. He allowed few initiatives over the years and never supervised or followed through. Power vacuums became filled by favorites whom Fr. Archie trusted; he held others in suspicion. And even though Fr. Archie was fiscally undisciplined, no one faced him with financial facts or their implications. That would have led only to an argument and the refrain.

In Fr. Archie's last year, the parish budget had to be cut by one-third. Full-time staff were offered a severance package because paying them was unsustainable. Staff members left exhausted, grieving, and resentful. They had enjoyed Fr. Archie's Friday homemade chili lunches and his inquiries about the health of their mothers, but they walked out the door uncertain about the genuineness of his care for them.

Fr. Archie had inherited a parish with a solid financial foundation and ministry structure. He left behind for his successor disconnected pieces and wide squabbling.

Why Lone Rangerism Fails

The lone ranger pastor may have limited skills, be a strong introvert, have rigid ideological commitments and authoritarian leanings, feel insecure and defensive, or be a combination of the above. All these dispositions inhibit synodality processes. While such a pastor may be holy, kind, charming, a good preacher, and even organized, the lone ranger mindset blocks the full implementation and effectiveness of synodality practices in the parish.

Why? Lone ranger pastoral leadership stimulates a stunting dynamic in a parish. Staff members and parishioners—whether for power or security—tend to reach toward what they perceive to be the pastor's preferences. Dialogue with the pastor on a personal or group level becomes impeded, nurturing competitive rivalry and manipulation in some while dispiriting and distancing others. Consequently, fog arises in decision-making and implementation. Conflict surfaces, thwarting the mission. Grief, apathy, and anger well up in the parish community.

Historical Notes

Acts of the Apostles 15:1-19, tells about the church's decision to shift its ministry in relationship with the gentiles. The presbyters and elders of Jerusalem gather. They listen and dialogue. Paul, James, and Peter—maestros each in their own ways—shape the decision-making. The whole group reaches agreement.

The letter from the Jerusalem church announcing the decisions to the gentile community at Antioch begins: "It is the decision of the Holy Spirit and of us…" That wording is stunning.

From Acts forward, the Church understands that group-based pastoral leadership works. Bishops form a college that gives unity and continuity to church teaching, including the Bishop of Rome within and above the college of bishops. Authoritative and consultative bodies across the church—ecumenical councils and bishops synods, diocesan presbyteral and deacons' councils, diocesan synods, parish councils, finance councils, and parish assemblies—mirror this same sensibility. Pastoral leadership centers itself in groups.

In the listening and discerning group, the Holy Spirit inspires, animates, directs, and leads the church with presence and power, and often with wind and fire.

A pastor on the synodal way leads by listening and dialoguing and must necessarily be skillful in groups. ∎

THE PASTOR

One Among Many

The Pastor, a Passing Pilgrim

Most pastors serve a term of office at the bishop's discretion. Many parishioners participate in a parish's life far longer than any given pastor, some for generations.

These realities suggest that pastors are not the bulwark of parish life. The parishioners abide as a parish's past, present, and future.

Moreover, each parish has a unique personality and culture. Even adjacent parishes differ because each is shaped by personalities, economics, the style and priorities of leadership, history, and the specifics of its location. During his tenure, a pastor can only partially grasp the fullness of a parish's personality and culture.

A pastor, therefore, needs to shape his ministry for the long haul, not the short run, and for the parishioners, not himself.

The Pastor as Power-Sharer

The first concern of a pastor, then, is to empower the staff and parishioners for participation and leadership in ministry.

A pastor can take for granted his institutionally established authority. Building trust, however, requires that a pastor strive to equip the people of the parish to fill their baptismal role in mission, that he works hard to enable all in the parish to fulfill their co-responsibility to serve and witness in Gospel ministry for the sake of the church's mission to the world.

Many pastors find parishioners hungry to participate but lacking clarity about their boundaries and feeling shy about exercising their proper role. Church and pastors can intimidate parishioners, who often lack basic information about how church works. Because parishioners are more American than Catholic, their outlook on leadership can be noisy and confused from the perspective of the Gospel and the Tradition.

A pastor willing to midwife the parishioners into effectively exercising their leadership while also honoring their history ignites gifts in a community that can fire deep parishioner participation in mission.

The Pastor as Co-Pastor

A pastor is likely to find professional staff members similarly hungry to lead but hampered by agendas rising out of hurt and disillusionment from their past service. Staff members are often wary of the pastor's authority, preoccupied with job security, and feeling less than fully trusting.

A pastor willing to receive the staff members' gifts, accept them, bless their ministry, express his thanks, and join with them in honoring their leadership and honing their skills nurtures life in staff members that can blossom forth in remarkable teamwork, glorious creativity, and astonishing ministry service.

The Pastor as Host and Guest

The pastor who listens instead of orders, coaches instead of demands, discerns with instead of talks at and encourages instead of insists extends rich hospitality to parishioners and staff. Such hospitality, over time, transforms the minds and hearts of a parish community.

If a pastor acts toward parishioners and staff as an attentive host who cares for their need and graciously accepts their offered gifts as a thankful guest, a pastor's hospitable ministry can serve as a critical key to transforming parish life.

The Pastor: a Professional Generalist

The urgency of parish demands and the allure of

the larger culture pressing against the lives of parishioners challenge a pastor's temptation to passivity about specific ministries, narrow specialty in ministry service, or time-consuming hobbies or gigs outside the parish. Our day and age calls pastors to maintain disciplined engagement in the larger Church and the parish, to focus on the mission, and to be broadly competent. That is, a pastor needs to be a dedicated generalist.

Staying a generalist means overseeing the parish, mindful of its context, in listening, dialoguing, discerning, and collaborative relationships with parishioners and leadership groups.

A pastor typically knows more people from more angles, more deeply, and more perceptively than staff members or parishioners, at least after the pastor has been in the saddle for four years or more. Pastors report that the level to which the parishioners admit them into their lives at the bedside of a loved one, in funeral preparation, at their dining room table, and in the pastor's office—often for good, occasionally with rancor—can be amazing to experience. Remaining a generalist honors the unique position a pastor holds and a pastor's singular perspective.

> I am a Christian for my own sake, whereas I am a leader for your sake.
>
> St. Augustine, *On Pastors*

A pastor's great strength rests in remaining the listening generalist, one community member among all, while yet using the natural gifts of being pastor to the parish's long-haul advantage for the sake of accomplishing the mission.

When Pastoring Works...

Over the years, teachers and parishioners often asked Fr. Cassian for a gym addition to the school building.

Fr. Cassian evaded the request. His four predecessors had failed, even though one went so far as to have plans drawn up. Having no sports interests, Fr. Cassian had little appreciation for the "need" for a gym. Moreover, year after year, the budget came in so tight that Fr. Cassian judged that a capital campaign was beyond the parish and himself.

Inside the classroom building one day during a fire drill, Fr. Cassian watched the children trip and stumble over a boy on crutches and then over one another because the back stairs were rickety and the exit too narrow. The drill also took twice as long as it ought to have taken. Fr. Cassian felt alarmed by the situation's danger.

Fr. Cassian raised his concerns to the councils. Before three years ended, with the consensus of both councils and wide parishioner support, the parish built a gym, meeting space, library, four classrooms, and parish offices onto the school building… and they were paying for it.

Under the pressure of a genuine safety concern, Fr. Cassian finally began to attune himself to the needs and desires of the parish community. Listening, dialoguing, and discerning with the community, Fr. Cassian grew beyond his fear and dismissive attitudes to offer the parish community the long-haul leadership they deserved.

The Pastor as Igniter of Participation

Effective pastoral leadership requires synodality practices: broad participation of the pastor, parishioners, and staff together in mission. Participation helps the pastor, staff, and parishioners together enjoy the mystery of the parish's history, personality, and culture even as it stimulates all of them together in growth toward a richer understanding and ever-fuller exercise of Gospel pastoral leadership.

This style of leadership—listening, dialoguing, discerning, making decisions, implementing them, evaluating them together, each as one among equals—builds trust among pastor, staff, and parishioners. A synodal leadership style strengthens everyone's commitment to the main engine for fulfilling the parish's mission: not the pastor alone, but the whole parish community. ■

THE PASTOR

Reflections for a Pastor

Synodal Style Works: A True Story

Fr. Jay inherited a parish his predecessor controlled with two cronies. He decided to take a long-haul view and a synodal approach to his pastoring.

Fr. Jay began by working hard to distribute power across staff and parishioners. He gave the pastoral and finance councils real authority to focus, guide, and monitor the parish's life, as well as plan its future. He brought real parish problems to the councils for their consideration, insisted on unanimous consent for decisions, and participated as an equal in council deliberations. All council decisions were entrusted to the Holy Spirit and considered under one question: what does God want of us?

Fr. Jay respected staff expertise and decision-making authority and consistently supported them publicly, confining disagreements to private conversations. He told the staff and the parish that whenever a staff member was present, the parish's pastoring ministry was in the room. He honored that statement in practice.

He encouraged focus group listening initiatives among school parents and parishioners; the councils used the resulting materials for planning. If people brought forward ideas, the councils processed them and gave the initiator direct feedback about leadership group responses.

Fr. Jay published a yearly financial report and the parish's budget, structuring the accounts in a way that made clear what each ministry in the parish cost, including his salary and living expenses. He published his weekly schedule. He instituted an annual anniversary celebration of the church's consecration, along with a dinner, and used the occasion to reflect with parishioners on the parish's history as a faith community and its contemporary implications.

Over 11 years, in a 900-household parish, ministry participation rose from 250 to 670 parishioners sharing time and talent. The parish retired $300,000 in debt, raised $350,000 more for school repairs, and built a ministry center on stewardship pledges alone.

Fr. Jay implemented this parish's synodal practices in fits and starts. He faced difficulties and trudged on through extended decision-making processes. He made mistakes and struggled with consistency.

Over the long haul, however, parish life deepened, faith commitment grew, and the parish accomplished far more than Fr. Jay ever expected as he began his pastorate. Ultimately, Fr. Jay could not imagine any other way of being Church for a parish.

Questions for Consideration

To embrace a synodal way of proceeding, pastoral leadership—the pastor in particular—and the parish leadership and assembly need to consider major questions. The questions below, framed for a pastor, might be framed for anyone in pastoral leadership:

* Is my first interest what I want for the parish? Am I willing to embrace community-shared desires instead?

* Am I willing to make my priority commitment to entrusting the parish's life to the gifts and power of the Holy Spirit wherever that leads?

* Am I willing to be transparent about parish ministry aims and plans? About finances and holdings?

* Am I committed to sharing my authority and power with community members?

* Am I willing to embrace listening as my fundamental posture toward the community and its leadership?

* Am I willing to embrace discernment as the parish way of decision-making?

* Am I willing to do the work or procure the right assistance to equip parish staff, leaders, and members for attentive listening and Spirit-filled discernment?

* Am I willing to structure effective power-sharing methods and processes with the pastoral council? With the finance council?

* Am I prepared to embrace equality with the parish's council members within decision-making processes?

* Am I committed to "What does God want of us?" unanimity within decision-making processes?

* Am I willing to respect ministry staff members as, effectively, co-pastors?

* Am I willing to engage in ongoing consultation with the parish assembly about parish vision, direction, and ministry evaluation?

* Am I prepared to be forthright about the limits of Church law and diocesan regulation within discernment processes? Am I open to discussion? To interceding on the parish's behalf?

* Am I willing and able to say "no" as well as "yes?"

* Can I be patient and merciful with messiness and conflict in meetings and with individuals?

* Can I patiently participate in listening and discerning processes so they have adequate time to mature for sound decision-making?

* Am I prepared to be forthright and publicly accountable about my perspectives and mistakes?

* Am I willing to defend a synodal way of proceeding to the bishop? To priests? To parish leadership and parishioners?

* Am I willing to lead to the peripheries to be faithful to Gospel mission?

COUNCIL BASICS

COUNCIL BASICS
Parish Councils in Law

Origin of a Pattern

From the beginning, the Church has gathered in groups to discern and receive the Holy Spirit's gifts. This tradition finds its grounding in Jesus' calling disciples, establishing the new Israel with the designation of the Twelve, and stories about the bestowal of the Holy Spirit.

This pattern continues as Peter gathers the disciples to elect Matthias one of the Twelve (Acts 2:15-26) and as leaders gather the community to elect assistants to wait on table (Acts 6:1-7), send Barnabas and Saul on mission (Acts 13:1-3), hear Paul's report about his missions (Acts 14:27), and shape new policy for opening to the gentiles (Acts 15:1-21).

These foundational experiences of the community gathering to access the Holy Spirit's power have inspired the Church throughout the ages to establish councils, synods, and assemblies of all sorts, trusting the Holy Spirit's power and movement within and among the Church gathered.

In our time, this traditional pattern motivates the Church, in law, to constitute two consulting groups in every parish for the pastor and parishioners to gather to discern the Spirit's gifts.

The Pastoral Council

The first parish consultation group is the pastoral council.

> If the diocesan bishop judges it opportune after he has heard the presbyteral council, a pastoral council is to be established in each parish; the pastor presides over it, and through it the Christian faithful along with those who share in the pastoral care of the parish in view of their office, give their help in fostering pastoral activity. This pastoral council possesses a consultative vote only and is governed by the norms determined by the diocesan bishop.
>
> Canon 536

This canon calls the pastor to consult with the pastoral council regarding:

* the focus, guidance, and monitoring of the parish's ministries (ministry commitments and structures, staff member numbers and job descriptions, and ministry evaluation);

* pastoral planning for the parish;

* any matter that warrants corporate review;

* the structuring, execution, and maintenance of parish-wide consultation processes; and

* all matters the pastor chooses to bring before it.

The pastoral council belongs to the pastor. It has no life of its own; it is united to the pastor's ministry and informs it. The pastoral council, therefore, ought never to be an adversarial body. Rather, it is a consultative body that exists in communion relationship with the pastor.

The pastoral council aims to help foster pastoral activity (ministry). A pastoral council aims to do the hard work of building consensus around a parish community's vision of Gospel ministry and its implementation. Implied: consensus is a gift of the Holy Spirit that the Church calls us to build within and across our faith communities so we grow in unity for Gospel mission.

> How necessary pastoral councils are! A bishops cannot guide a diocese without pastoral councils. A priest cannot guide without pastoral councils.
>
> Pope Francis, Assisi, October 4, 2013

The Finance Council

Canon law mandates a second consultation group universally.

> Each parish is to have a finance council which is regulated by universal law as well as by norms issued by the diocesan bishop; in this council the Christian faithful, selected according to the same norms, aid the pastor in administration of parish goods.
>
> Canon 537

This canon calls the pastor to consult with the finance council about:

* the focus, guidance, and monitoring of the parish's administration ministries:
  * finances (budget, financial stewardship, gifts of money and stock),
  * property (buildings, grounds, and gifts of real estate),
  * personnel (salaries and benefits), and
  * law (personnel policies and the disposition of parish property)
* the yearly budget, financial stewardship, endowment fund maintenance and distribution, property management, and development;
* any matter that warrants corporate review; and
* all matters brought before it regarding personnel and law.

That this canon immediately follows the other tells us that the finance and pastoral councils are parallel entities. The finance council, like the pastoral council, belongs to the pastor.

Because of its mission, the finance council requires members who have legal and financial expertise, even if members with such expertise come from outside the parish. To preserve collegiality, the membership of a finance council must also be, at minimum, three persons beyond the pastor.

Since the goods of the parish belong to the parish itself, not the pastor, finance council transparency to the whole parish community is of extremely high value.

The Inter-Council Relationship

Each council has a distinct purpose. Their divergent responsibilities imply that each group is comprised of different persons. The pastor links the councils. He presides over each.

While practical wisdom suggests structuring even broader linkage between the councils, the law indicates that the shape of that connection depends upon the pastor.

PRINCIPLES FOR EFFECTIVE TWO-COUNCIL FUNCTION:

* The pastoral council is the parish's ultimate decision-making body.
* Finance council recommendations deserve consummate respect.
* In times of disagreement, bring both councils together for listening, dialogue, discernment, and decision-making.

The Pastor and the Councils

The law implies that the pastor is not apart from but participates with each council. That means that the pastor shapes the agenda, sets the extent and limits of council decisions, provides maximum information to the councils so they can offer the best consultation possible, and partners with council members in the movement toward consensus.

Both councils aim to exercise pastor and parishioner co-responsibility and accountability by listening, dialogue, discernment, consensual decision-making, and evaluation of Gospel ministry.

COUNCIL BASICS

The Councils' Mission

The Parish's Mission

When he reorganized the Diocese of Rome, Pope Francis clarified the missionary aim of the diocese. His words bear careful consideration.

According to Pope Francis' genius, the aim of a diocese, and a parish by extension, is to "be primarily an exemplary place of communion, dialogue and proximity, welcoming and transparent, at the service of… renewal and pastoral growth… an evangelizing community, a synodal Church, a people which credibly witness to God's mercy" (*In Ecclesiarum Communione*, Pope Francis, January 7, 2023).

The Pope would have every activity within a diocese and a parish, at whatever level and with whatever degree of responsibility, be "always by its nature pastoral, oriented according to synodal style."

Councils for a parish, therefore, aim not merely at ecclesiastical organization. Their purpose is to fulfill the missionary aspiration of the Church with the express intention of reaching everyone.

Councils within the Mission

To this end, the councils' purpose is to properly shape the parish's mission locally and build parish community consensus around its mission's particular contours.

The linkage between the councils is at the discretion of the pastor. Ordinarily, however, the following principles practically apply:

* Each council is comprised of different persons who serve each council's distinct mission.

* Because its focus is the broad range of Gospel ministries in the parish, the pastoral council serves as the parish's ultimate consensus-building consultation body.

* It is wise for the pastor to ask the pastoral council to review significant finance council matters—notably the yearly budget and all corporation-related decisions—to build consensus in the parish.

* In a pastoral council review, finance council recommendations deserve consummate respect and every benefit of the doubt.

* During a time of disagreement between the councils about a major parish matter (the yearly budget, erection of a building, hiring a new staff member, etc.), growing toward consensus among parish leadership and the whole community requires that the councils be brought together to enter into a discernment process and establish a joint consensus decision.

Journeying Toward Conversion and Transformation

Parish life in all its facets—worship, religious education, spiritual formation, pastoral care, community building, and the ministries of charity, justice, and administration—endeavors to call people to know Jesus Christ, to grow in mature adult faith, to bear witness to God's mercy, and to reach out to accompany in mercy those on the peripheries of the parish's life.

The rationale for every element of parish life, therefore, needs to be inviting people to a loving, committed relationship with Jesus Christ and conversion to the pattern of life Jesus has shown us.

A faithful synodal way of proceeding for the parish and its consultative groups invites the members of the parish community to be what we preach… within parish life and beyond it.

The parish's councils have a critical leadership role in fulfilling the mission.

COUNCIL BASICS

Planning and the Pastoral Council

Pastoral Ministry Planning

"Where there is no vision, the people perish," says one translation of Proverbs 29:18. A compelling vision wakes people up, rouses their enthusiasm, and focuses their energy toward forward movement. The first task of the pastor and councils together is to offer the parish vision.

Vision requires planning.

Planning is the backbone of council ministry. Planning gives contour and thrust to the parish's forward movement as it strives to reach consensus about its identity, image, characteristics, and direction. Pastoral planning managed by the councils and coordinated across all parish leadership groups is vital to the ongoing life of a parish community.

The Pastoral Council and Planning

The pastoral council serves as the parish's essential planning group. Because its charge is ministry vision, the pastoral council's planning mandate is the steel spine that holds its process together. Thus, planning is the top priority for the pastoral council and the engine for its meetings.

If other matters intervene—they always do—the planning process pauses to accommodate them. Approving the yearly budget, discussing the rising crisis, debriefing the bishop's pastoral visit, and sorting through the pastor's latest personnel quandary continually interrupt the planning flow. That reality must be an accepted part of the pastoral council's process.

Nonetheless, pastoral ministry planning is the task that holds everything together for the pastoral council.

> It is the function of the pastoral council to investigate everything pertaining to pastoral activities, to weigh them carefully, and to set forth practical conclusions concerning them so as to promote conformity of the life and actions of the People of God with the Gospel.
>
> Pope St. Paul VI, August 6, 1966

The Planning Process

An effective pastoral council follows a good planning process. Whatever process might be selected, it needs to be clear, complete, carefully articulated, easy to follow, and promising for the results the council seeks.

A poor planning process leaves in its wake a rather chunky stew, both in people's minds and on paper, and neither staff nor parishioners will be able to grab hold of it or use it.

The process that works will be the process that outlines explicit goals and specific tasks for particular persons and groups accomplish at precise time intervals with accountable results. Nothing less is worth the council's time and effort.

Writing a good five-year plan will take the pastoral council, in collaboration with the finance council, parish commissions and committees, and the parish assembly, 18 months or more. This time frame is ordinary. A highly participative process, including the gathering of accurate data, focus group discussions, and ministry commission and parish assembly input, requires generous time if it is to be a consensus-building process for pastoral leadership and the whole parish.

The critical insight that the implementing of synodality practices invites us to ponder is this: the process of planning—its focus, breadth, listening, discernment process, level of whole parish participation, outreach to the peripheries, and continuing refreshment based on the concrete realities of parish life—is far more important than a document when it comes to planning.

THE LISTENING PARISH

After a pastoral plan is published, a monitoring and evaluation process will demand continuing and extensive pastoral council involvement with parish staff, ministry commissions and committees, the parish assembly, and those on the margins of parish life. As major parish projects outside the plan arise, the pastoral plan requires revision.

The Parapet Surprise

Fr. Richard began his pastorate focused on planning, and he invited the pastoral council into an extended planning process. Because the council members were inexperienced and their time was kept carefully limited, planning began as a trudge. Nonetheless, beliefs, a mission statement, and functions emerged from the process over several months and were shared with the finance council, staff, and parish. The process grew in momentum and parish support.

Just when the planning process began assessing parish resources, the maintenance coordinator found a brick on the ground in front of the school entry. When he looked up and saw it had fallen from high on the front façade, he immediately contacted Earl, the chair of the maintenance committee. A construction engineer, Earl, toured the school roof. After consulting with Fr. Richard, who had to look up the word parapet, Earl arranged for a team of engineers to assess the whole brick and cement parapet. Their conclusion: the entire parapet—three feet tall around the whole school building—was bowing out and falling. It needed to be replaced immediately. The cost? $350,000.

The front entry to the school was cordoned off. Fr. Richard and Earl met with the councils.

The pastoral council set aside long-range planning to arrange a capital campaign for paying off the debt and the new construction. The project included both councils' consensus to hire a part-time development director to shape a multi-layered publicity campaign for the parish and public-at-large, to frame up fundraising, and to follow through on the gift-giving process, from interviewing through meetings to mailings through thank yous. All this activity took months to plan and execute.

Meanwhile, the old parapet was gently taken down and a simpler replacement was installed.

The pastoral council had to set aside the planning process for several months. When the council took it up again, however, the parapet surprise had affirmed the beliefs, mission, and functions statement already done even as the whole process had reshaped the council members' and Fr. Richard's understanding of the parish's true resources.

The Planning Process Structures an Unending Orientation

A parish's pastoral plan document frames a community's orientation. The document is not law. The planning process constitutes the experience of Church, not the document.

In an ever-changing world, continual listening to the parish community's real pastoral need, attending to the gifts and demands of the Gospel call to mercy that manifest themselves with time, discerning an effective response to that need, then implementing and evaluating. This is the ministry work that infuses the structured process of planning with meaning. The process is the point.

Consequently, the usual five-year planning cycle, including the ever-messy interventions of reality that intrude, never ends, and it shouldn't.

Pastoral planning is the backbone of the pastoral council process. Planning is the pastoral council's first responsibility as a wise vision keeper for the parish and its ongoing task as the consensus-building engine for a parish community's Gospel ministry. ■

COUNCIL BASICS

Planning and the Finance Council

Ministry Planning

All parish planning gives contour and thrust to the parish's forward movement. All planning for the parish, therefore, is pastoral. That is, all planning, under the umbrella of listening to the people's hearts under the question "What does God want of us?" strives to discern and implement God's desires for a parish community as it seeks to fulfill its Gospel mandate.

The process of coordinated, engaged, community-wide, ongoing planning remains vital to the life of a parish community.

The Finance Council and Planning

The parish's finance council focuses its activities in partnership with the pastoral council's planning process and the whole parish's mission.

Expert in legal, financial, personnel, and infrastructure matters, the finance council listens and discerns what is required for the parish to remain secure practically, legally, and financially for the parish's long-range future flourishing.

These overarching responsibilities demand that the finance council, in a practical way, spend its time monitoring financial giving and income/expense trends, fashioning the short- and long-term budget and maintenance schedules, and discerning what direction parish resource development ought to take.

Structured to be a parish community's wise vision keeper regarding infrastructure, resources, personnel, and security, the finance council, too, aims to build consensus around the parish's Gospel mission vision.

> All the goods that we have, the Lord gives them to go to the world, to go to humanity, to help others.
>
> Pope Francis, October 21, 2013

Task-Oriented

Planning alongside the pastoral council serves as the backbone of the parish's finance council.

Because the finance council attends to money and property, its process is less shaped by a formal structure, like a set long-range planning process, than it is by the council's singular tasks:

✸ writing or at least approving the yearly financial report,

✸ constructing the stewardship appeal,

✸ pulling together the annual budget,

✸ reviewing monthly and quarterly financial statements,

✸ responding to the periodic building maintenance surprise,

✸ shaping and overseeing capital expenses,

✸ determining yearly endowment distributions, and

✸ constructing the upcoming capital campaign.

Sometimes regularly, other times in fits and starts, concrete tasks govern finance council planning.

Discernment and Decision-Making

Finance councils need to rely on the same discernment process as the pastoral council.

> The finance council fulfills a role of particular importance in the growth, at the level of the parish community, of a culture of co-responsibility, of administrative transparency, and of service to the needs of the Church.
>
> *The Pastoral Conversion of the Parish Community in the Service of the Evangelizing Mission of the Church*

The nature of its concerns, however, leads to a more informal decision-making process. Money discussions can be intense but may require no significant decisions. Maintenance surprises can lead to review and hand-wringing or censure, but the fix generally solves problems, and a payment amount is often out of a council's control. Eyes glaze over when faced with fuzzy financial reporting; such reporting can elicit brisk questioning from pastors and parishioners. Still, reports typically require tweaking, not overhaul. Fiscal long-range planning that projects into a second year stands as a tentative business. Planning beyond three years is nigh a waste of time.

The budget approval process, building facilities, or setting in place a capital campaign typically demand the most discernment work for a finance council. Personnel issues can do so as well. Most often, however, only the budget is a yearly, frequent-meeting process.

Collaborating with the Pastoral Council

A critical principle to remember is that the pastoral and finance councils are complementary pastoral leadership groups. The councils depend on one another for their effective functioning.

The finance council, often tempted to go it alone based only on numbers, constructs the budget according to pastoral council and parish assembly priorities. The finance council's money and property recommendations, often accepted as-is by a pastoral council, need to align with a pastoral council's planning goals. Whatever the case, finance council recommendations may go forward only with the pastoral council's approval.

At the same time, the pastoral council must be mindful that members will often be tempted to shrug their shoulders over concerns that have oppressed the finance council. The dialogue between the two councils needs to be substantive, wide-ranging, and thorough.

In its practical functioning, the finance council intuitively feels like a highly technical subcommittee of the pastoral council. Peace holds sway between the councils, however, when every care is taken to treat them as parallel entities and when they come together in respectful agreement as peers. ■

COUNCIL BASICS

Council Election & Eligibility

What is "Election"?

The ecclesial concept of election to leadership differs from the common assumptions of a democracy: running for office, secret ballot, and majority rule. The ecclesial notion of election modifies those assumptions markedly.

Democracy-Style Elections Are Not the Synodal Way

For setting accurate expectations in a pastoral leadership group, a democratic style of council election is least suitable. Even the word *election* means something different in the democratic context, where the word refers largely to a "running for office" process and specifically to the results of the casting of ballots.

Democratic-style election in a parish runs the risk of bringing people into leadership who are focused on representation rather than communion, checks and balances rather than participation, and legislation rather than discernment. These suppositions can create a drag on a parish leadership group's process and even open conflict.

Ancient Church "Election" Traditions

Whether the position be pope, patriarch, or abbot, *election* in Church traditions is, first, the results of the process of discerning the eligibility of a person for an office—more like nomination in the American sense.

Second, except in rare cases, the selection of an office holder requires more than majority rule. The aim of election in a church setting is consensus. Consequently, except for extenuating circumstances, a two-thirds majority is most often required for selection for ecclesial office.

In the Church, people never run for office. Instead, they are, in some form, nominated. Their qualifications are discussed by the group, either as a whole gathered (abbot) or on the side (pope), in a prayerful discernment process. A person's interest in holding the office is typically assessed within the discernment of eligibility process.

The balloting process, typically repeated, is a structured and prayerful part of the discernment process that leads to selection.

Council Leadership Eligibility

Consequently, consideration of an election process in a parish begins with eligibility requirements. That is, clear expectations make good council members. Clarity demands that eligibility requirements for council membership be made widely known in the parish.

The box below articulates requirements for council leadership consistent with synodal practices and the models explored above and below.

---

* Registered parishioner.
* Participation in Sunday Eucharist.
* Understanding that the council belongs to the pastor.
* Support of the current council processes.
* A three-year commitment.
* Faithful attendance at a maximum of two 1½ hour meetings per month for 10 months.
* Commitment to careful listening.
* Participation in discussion.
* Commitment to prayerful discernment about the parish's ministry and its future.
* The ability to keep confidences.

A Discernment Election Process

In a parish setting, especially one following synodal practices, discernment-oriented election to a council position is consistent with the parish's values and practice.

The process begins with publishing the eligibility requirements. It then proceeds with mustering candidates for election.

Some parishes enter a process of community-wide prayer and reflection in which some people are recommended, and others are personally moved to come forward. Other parishes begin the process with a council discussion, then call for volunteers in the bulletin, tap people on the shoulder, or ask people whose name surfaces if they are interested in serving.

Methods vary. Critically, the method chosen aims to match the eligibility qualifications with potential, capable candidates. This process is a form of "election."

Next, the "elect" are interviewed to discern their interest and suitability. The interview also aims to clarify mutual expectations, which is key to the process. Thus, the eligibility requirements are thoroughly discussed in the interviews.

The interviewers might be the pastor, or include the pastor, or pastoral or finance council members.

Often the interviews result in just enough candidates to fill open slots. With that, the process of selection is complete.

If more candidates are available than slots, the candidates may offer themselves for balloting by the parish assembly. Overseen by the pastoral council, a ranked selection process would be most suitable for balloting.

Pastoral Council Versus Finance Council Election

Election to a pastoral council differs from that to a finance council.

Finance council ministry requires a technical interest, expertise, and experience unnecessary for pastoral council ministry. Consequently, parishes feel blessed to even find five finance council members to elect.

Nine pastoral council members—three new each year—are most often easy to muster.

COUNCIL MEETINGS

COUNCIL MEETINGS

Effective Council Meetings

The pastoral and finance councils serve as conduits for the Holy Spirit's work in the parish. They also serve as a training ground for exercising synodality practices. Council effectiveness in accomplishing ordinary business and developing synodal leadership requires two complementary elements for council meetings: stout content and effective process.

Stout Meeting Content

Four rules of thumb govern meeting content:

* **The pastor invites the councils to make real decisions that focus, guide, and monitor the parish's ministry life.** Parish ministry planning, hiring of staff, sudden staff reduction, salary raise proposals, the rectory budget, capital expense planning, the stewardship appeal theme, and presenters—all large, directional parish concerns need to be brought to the appropriate council for review and decision.

* **The group receives everything it needs to make good decisions.** Information sharing makes or breaks decision-making. Everyone, therefore, needs to be given all the relevant data for review. Objective details, thorough and unvarnished, are necessary for informed and balanced decision-making. When in doubt, share the information. If the pastor needs confidentiality, ask it.

* **Careful decision-making requires that the pastor trust the council with confidential material.** If the council or leadership group knows only some details, it will make ill-informed and unreliable decisions. Full decisions require full disclosure and transparency.

* **Meeting prayer is both simple and substantive.** All council considerations fall under the umbrella question: What does God want of us? The conscience question "Can I live with this decision?" serves as the bottom line for each participant personally and the whole group. Meeting process, therefore, requires simple prayer and some creativity about prayer's form and timing.

Effective Meeting Process

The meeting aims to open to the Holy Spirit's gifts. Effective meeting process requires that the leader and group understand these rules:

* Council leadership requires commitment. When members cannot attend, they communicate that to a designated person before a meeting.

* Participants come on time. If a meeting starts promptly, the group accomplishes more, and the session ends on time.

* Participants receive an agenda before the meeting, at least one day before. The agenda is reviewed and modified by agreement as the session begins.

* The pastor participates as an equal in the council's entire process.

* All council members listen. Reciprocal listening shapes every discussion and offers rich food for the process.

* All council members participate fully and forthrightly in the discussion. The parish needs the best thinking of everyone to serve the parish well.

* All words shared pass through three gates. The first gate is truth. All words must be true. The second gate is necessity. All words must be necessary. The third gate is kindness. All words must be kind. Participants always do well to remember the three gates.

* Council members share honestly. If members have a personal agenda, they need to be frank about that or drop it. Seeking what God

wants for the parish is about submission to the Holy Spirit's power, not fulfilling personal agendas.

✱ Council members honor what other participants offer: introverted or extroverted, a gift for chairing, for subcommittee work, or hospitality. All gifts are honored.

✱ Council members "bat the camel on the nose." If a participant is troubled by another, then he or she ought to deal with the concern forthrightly and kindly outside the group. If a group member sees bothersome patterns arising within the group, then he or she raises the concern and asks the group to talk about them, and the group honors the request. Batting the camel on the nose prevents the whole smelly camel from entering the tent.

✱ Council members ponder: what can I live with? The council's process is spiritual and aimed toward unanimity. If someone cannot live with a decision, the group needs to listen, dialogue, and pray until it discerns a consensus direction.

✱ Council members carefully review confidentiality expectations. The ability to share confidential material allows the pastor and council members to speak freely and securely, enables the council to make well-informed decisions, and permits the council to take what time it needs to decide without interference.

✱ The pastor and council members publicly affirm and support consensus decisions. In meetings, people will argue points of view, but when council members leave the room, they stand by the consensus achieved and explain it with clarity and enthusiasm.

✱ Decisions are implemented. The proof of trust rests in the follow-up. If the decision is right and good, it must be followed to the letter and its effects monitored. If observation and listening suggest that a decision is questionable, it needs to be brought back to the council for review.

✱ The agenda for the next meeting is decided and agreed upon—mindful that things come up—at the end of the session.

✱ A summary report of the meeting is shared with the participants, the pastor, the staff, and the parish assembly.

When the Process Goes Awry

Eddie was a trustee who disagreed with Fr. Derrick's handling of a property concern with a parish neighbor. The finance and pastoral councils had discussed the matter several times as a pastor's report. Unfortunately, the pastor and councils failed to appreciate the magnitude of parish concern, and council members soft-pedaled their opinions because of Fr. Derrick's apparent strength of conviction.

Also, unfortunately, Eddie raised his disapproval in the parish rather than with Fr. Derrick or within the council meetings. Taking a false cue and complicating that reserve, fellow finance council members withheld their honest opinions when Eddie was in the room. They let a sleeping wolf lie.

Fr. Derrick eventually received frank council member opinions, but outside the meetings and accompanied by hand-wringing about community damage being done by Eddie's public complaints.

The property matter remained poorly handled for many months. Hurt and angry, Eddie resigned from the finance council and as a parish trustee.

The Equality of Process and Content

When weighty Gospel ministry concerns combine with effective, efficient, spiritually based processes, listening, dialogue, and prayer typically bring about the channeling of the Spirit's gifts. That's how a council discerns what God wants for a parish and from it for the sake of authentic, co-responsible, and accountable Gospel ministry… and sometimes plain good order. ■

COUNCIL MEETINGS

The Place of Confidentiality

The Building of Trust

Complete information exchange, thorough discussion, good counsel, and balanced decision-making require council members and staff members to keep confidence with the pastor and one another. Secure confidentiality offers the pastor the opportunity to share information at length and in-depth so the councils and staff can make sound, evenhanded recommendations. Respect for confidentiality offers a council and staff members the assurance that what they say in dialogue will not be bandied about or judged in the parish community. It also frees a council's and staff's process to be deep and wide-ranging.

Lack of confidentiality within a parish council or staff

* boxes them out of some decisions,
* inhibits making fully reasonable decisions,
* undercuts trust, and
* diminishes the council's and staff's effectiveness all around.

Is Confidentiality Secrecy?

Confidentiality differs from secrecy. Secrets concern the withholding of information in the moral realm. Secrets are never part of council or staff decisions. Confidential information, however, is part of many effective council and staff meetings.

Confidentiality Defined

Confidentiality means:

* holding specified information within a particular and designated network of persons (the council or staff)
* for the sake of the common good of persons in the group or groups.

The aim of council and staff decision-making processes is the common good, which sometimes demands that some issues be kept confidential. Typically, these matters include information relating to personnel, law, finances, and some relationship issues that need to be shared in a group. Hence, its members have fuller understanding within a discernment process, and the listening and dialogue ends with a completely considered decision.

Confidentiality also stands as an act of faith. Coming from the Latin *cum* (with) and *fides* (faith), confidentiality presumes within it a deep trust. In pastoral decision-making, it presumes trust that decision-making rests in God's hands and that God's work will be done through honoring fellow decision-makers—protecting their points of view and their process of changing them until decisions are reached.

What Does it Mean to Keep a Matter Confidential?

Keeping a matter confidential means that council or staff members share confidential material with no one. This standard must be met by every council member and staff member when confidentiality is asked.

The one exception for sharing confidences might be the council or staff member's spouse. Couples have different expectations of one another in this area; whatever their expectations, they ought to be respected. However, if a member shares confidential council information with a spouse, then the spouse, too, must keep the same confidence the council member keeps.

When a Confidence is Broken

The breaking of council or staff confidences—either by the member or a spouse—may require that

THE LISTENING PARISH

a council member be asked to leave the council.

Note: if a spouse breaks confidence, the council member is responsible.

Clearly Label Confidential Material

Keeping confidence requires that the pastor name clearly on the agenda and in the meeting any matters that are executive session, that is, matters to be kept confidential.

Ordinarily, the issues to be kept confidential for the sake of the common good of the parish are as follows:

* matters of persons and their relationships,
* parish benefactor information,
* all personal salary matters,
* detailed matters of personnel discipline and termination,
* some issues revealed within hiring,
* certain parish legal matters,
* the meeting exchanges of council or staff members, and
* the meeting discussion of controversial issues not yet decided (budget, etc.).

A parish's charitable concern for people and just concern about matters of personnel, law, finances, and property are the prisms through which a pastor or a council or staff member might consider what information ought to be shared and what ought to be kept confidential.

Confidentiality Can Be Awkward…

Fr. Placid, a relatively new pastor, watched quietly as a school ministry commission completed a smoke-and-mirrors budget that kept tuition unrealistically low.

Afterwards, the principal came to Fr. Placid and protested, "If we go down next year, and we will with this budget, it will hurt us irreparably. We've got to redo it." Over the next two days, they did. Fr. Placid then called an executive session school commission meeting to present the redone budget.

During the discussion, the commission reached consensus around a modified budget. But one person publicly indicated he wanted to speak with another parishioner before making a final decision, threatening to break executive session confidentiality. When that was pointed out to him, despite group pressure, he dug in.

Since consensus was blocked and breach of confidentiality was threatened, Fr. Placid told the school commission that he and the principal would decide the school's budget, submit it to the finance and pastoral councils, and inform the commission later about the result.

After the meeting, Fr. Placid took the commission member aside and told him—to his wide-eyed amazement—that if he broke confidentiality, he would forfeit his seat on the commission.

Fr. Placid ultimately kept the situation calm by implementing the redone budget that the commission—and even the difficult member—was ready to approve. Clear group rules, to which the commission had consented, allowed Fr. Placid to move as he did to preserve the common good.

Bottom Line

Every effort must be made to minimize confidential material so that decision-making processes may be as open as possible. This principle is especially important for a parish implementing synodality practices.

Indeed, fashioning a pastoral ministry response to the peripheries ordinarily fails to raise questions of confidentiality.

When questions of confidentiality do arise, however, the risk of sharing information in designated leadership groups and asking for confidentiality is worth it for two reasons:

* full information brings enormous benefit to discernment decision-making,
* and trust builds mightily from keeping the rules and keeping confidences.

COUNCIL MEETINGS
Meeting Agendas

Establishing an Agenda

The importance of a well-thought-out agenda, sent to meeting participants beforehand, along with its supporting documentation, cannot be overstated. Setting a proper agenda is half of any meeting's accomplishment. Experience teaches that whoever controls the agenda controls the meeting.

A synodal approach would suggest that the next meeting agenda items are best agreed upon at the end of the current meeting. Further items may need to be submitted in between sessions.

The council develops its sense of the pastor's and the chair's openness to transparency and accountability through the agenda assembly process, which either builds trust or undercuts it.

An Agenda Story

Sr. Mary was the parish's pastoral minister. She habitually submitted agenda items that raised questions better addressed in a brief meeting with the pastor. For over a year, whenever Sr. Mary presented "off the mark" items, the pastor would discuss them with her personally, clarifying why they were inappropriate for the agenda.

Gradually, Sr. Mary's discussions with the pastor in one-to-one meetings became more direct, and the off-the-mark agenda submissions ceased. The discussions between Sr. Mary and the pastor ultimately emerged as primary trust builders for Sr. Mary and the pastor in their relationship. It turned out that her hesitancy to trust the pastor had been the unspoken reason Sr. Mary submitted the off-beat items.

The Shape of an Agenda

All agenda items are assigned a discussion time so the chair can determine as the meeting progresses what business can best be accomplished and what could wait. Discussion sometimes requires choosing priorities. Time allotment not only structures the meeting but alerts participants to the anticipated depth of an item's discussion.

What's Not on the Agenda

Some matters need to be kept off the agenda: those that can be handled between two group members, items that are one person's responsibility, and items that put someone on the spot or are calculated to irritate.

If such matters arise, the person to whom the meeting belongs should talk to the submitter of the item about why it will not appear.

Sending Out the Agenda

If the pastor does not chair the council meeting, the agenda needs to be reviewed by the pastor before the agenda is sent out. The agenda ought to be in the hands of each council member at least two days before the meeting's scheduled time. ■

COUNCIL MEETINGS

Meeting Mechanics

Meetings Schedule

Effective pastoral council work requires that meetings be scheduled every other week for ten months a year. This scheduling gives the group time and momentum enough to get somewhere in pastoral planning. Given holidays and summers, that results in about 18 meetings a year.

Monthly meetings for a finance council are suitable for reports and planning, except perhaps during budget time, when more frequent meetings may be required because of budget details and time constraints.

Meeting Summary, Not Minutes

Meetings have no minutes. Recording meeting discussion is unnecessary. Instead, meeting summaries record only the decisions made at the meetings. A terse summary of reports can be helpful.

A brief listing of decisions and bottom-line report results ought to accompany the next meeting's agenda when it is sent out.

The parish files should attach these summaries to the meeting agenda in a file folder for a permanent record.

Meeting summaries may also be published in the bulletin. Share at least a summary of the summary with the whole parish assembly. Then listen!

Public Versus Executive Session Meetings

The pastoral and finance councils technically serve the discernment of the pastor's leadership of the parish's ministry. Council meetings are about communion, not representation, participation, not checks and balances, and discernment, not majority rule. Effective counsel for the pastor requires the sharing of confidential material at many meetings.

The councils stand as a first clearing house for pastoral ministry concerns that arise in the parish, and the councils typically determine how to co-responsibly and accountably handle these concerns in the wider community.

The pastor and council members coming to communion consensus about the parish's ordinary ministry business and how to process major arising pastoral ministry concerns can be a conflictual and messy process.

Consequently, council meetings ought not be public events. The reasoning for executive session meetings should be explained regularly to the parish community. ■

COUNCIL MEETINGS

Meeting Facilitation

Meeting Prayer

The Holy Spirit's presence and power are invoked in prayer at the start of every meeting. God always receives the glory at a meeting's end.

FORMS OF PRAYER

Some parishes begin council meetings with an extended reflection on the Sunday readings. Others pray briefly. Yet others invite participants to take turns offering prayer. Still others group-share petitionary prayer.

All these ways of praying can work. Some, however, take time and either extend the meeting or limit the possibilities of the meeting's work. Other methods stand as an imposition and are uncomfortable, especially for the introverted.

Originating in the monastic tradition, an ancient and venerable understanding of prayer is that it is like hurling javelins to the heavens. The image well-characterizes what council prayer ought best to look like.

LET PRAYER BE BRIEF!

At the meeting start, a brief and relatively formula-oriented prayer puts most people at ease and serves the meeting's purpose well. This prayer form can be instructive and moving when mindful of the liturgical year.

The meeting should always end with the briefest of prayers, a set formula. Everyone wants to get home. The doxology, "Glory be to the Father…" works exceptionally well. People respond instantly and automatically, the prayer is appropriate, and the praying says to a group of tired people: "The End."

Meeting Start

Every meeting begins with brief information sharing to put everyone at ease and dispel concerns beyond those on the agenda. The chair then

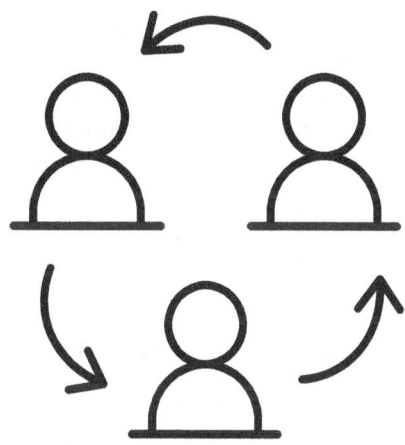

offers the group a brief overview of the agenda, which allows members to offer caveats based on unknowns or new information. It also gleans for the chair informal consent to what is to come.

The Meat of the Meeting

The chair begins each agenda item with a brief contextual introduction. Meeting participants need reminders about what agenda items mean for the parish and Gospel ministry. Developing item context saves time in discussions because people forget where an item comes from, how it fits, what it is connected to, why it is important, or why it needs to be discussed at this time.

Meeting Breaks

Ordinarily, a 90-minute time frame for pastoral and finance council meetings precludes break times. However, circumstances may arise when the chair might call for a break:

* A personal reflection and prayer break might assist the consensus process.
* A time out when a controversial conversation becomes too heated.
* A rest period after an intense processing segment of a meeting.

THE LISTENING PARISH

In all cases, a break should be only long enough to serve the meeting's purpose and short enough to avoid hobbling meeting momentum.

Meeting Length

Nothing worthwhile happens in a meeting beyond 90 minutes. Long meetings tire people out, drain their energy, and lead to fuzzy thinking, crankiness, manipulation, and bad decisions.

If a meeting extension is necessary to complete discussion, then group permission should be sought. If given, the extension ought to be less than 15 minutes. Failed consensus permission means the meeting ends on time.

Meeting Wind-Down

The meeting approaches its landing ten minutes before the projected end time. By five minutes before the projected meeting ends, the last three always-stable agenda items are reviewed.

* The chair summarizes the meeting, which allows the group to offer clarifying and forward-moving observations that sharpen agenda planning.

* The chair asks about the agenda next time. Consent about the following agenda bolsters group participation for the next meeting, affirms the group members' value and simplifies agenda assembly work.

* The chair affirms the date, time, and place of the next meeting. If meetings are scheduled in advance, this task is simple. If not, it may require some processing time.

Guests at Meetings

Occasionally, a pastoral or finance council meeting may require that a guest be present to offer expertise, perspective, or clarity to an agenda item.

A council meeting agenda ought to be framed to accommodate a guest conveniently. The presence of a guest would ordinarily be limited to designated agenda items, with the visitor noted on the agenda.

Hospitality to a council guest includes:

* welcoming the guest promptly,

* fully availing the council of the guest's contribution by providing ample time,

* bringing the guest's segment of the meeting to a distinct end,

* thanking the guest,

* and allowing the guest to leave as soon as their contribution is concluded.

The guest's withdrawal would ordinarily require a brief break before taking up the next agenda item or concluding a meeting.

COUNCIL MEETINGS

Who Chairs the Meeting?

Chairing Requires Competence

Competent chairmanship of a meeting is an acquired skill. The meeting chair makes or breaks the good experience of the participants during the session, council camaraderie, and meeting effectiveness.

So, two questions about meeting chairmanship deserve reflection: Who chairs council meetings? What does effective chairing look like?

> If the diocesan bishop judges it opportune after he has heard the presbyteral council, a pastoral council is to be established in each parish; the pastor presides over it…
>
> Canon 536

> Each parish is to have a finance council which is regulated by universal law as well as by norms issued by the diocesan bishop; in this council the Christian faithful, selected according to the same norms, aid the pastor in administration of parish goods.
>
> Canon 537

> The pastor represents the parish in all juridic affairs in accord with the norm of law…
>
> Canon 532

The Pastor Chairs if Possible, But…

In a church setting, the chair for a meeting ought best to be the person to whom the meeting "belongs." For a pastoral council, Canon 536 specifies that the pastor "presides." Regarding a finance council, the canon fudges a little. Nonetheless, it implies that the pastor presides.

Tidiness suggests, consequently, that the proper pastoral council or finance council meeting chair is the pastor.

Selecting a chair other than the pastor risks distorting the meeting and setting up the chair for embarrassment, manipulation, or failure. Clean lines of authority and accountability suggest that group meeting leadership follow the natural line of responsibility.

It's About Dignity and Mutual Respect

Like the parish pastoral council for a pastor, a diocesan presbyteral council belongs to the bishop. Henry Alphonse was bishop of a Midwestern U.S. diocese for 20 years. Widely respected as a formidable administrator who cared for his priests, he could be brisk about business and was nothing if not a straight shooter.

Though a bishop is technically, according to canon law, the "president" of the presbyteral council, each year, the presbyters of Bishop Alphonse's diocese—as is true for most dioceses—elected a presbyter whose primary task was to chair presbyteral council meetings.

In Bishop Alphonse's diocese, the council members sat at high, long tables around the room, leaving a large, open space in the center. The elected chair of the meeting always sat in the middle of one side. Bishop Alphonse always sat in the middle of the opposite side, facing the chair.

Many a presbyteral council chair sweat profusely as he tried to manage an unwieldy and outspoken crowd through a jammed agenda with Bishop Alphonse's every glance and gesture controlling him—often unwittingly, sometimes not—from across the room. The elected chair's discomfort was painful to observe, the very definition of a "hot seat."

The Most Competent Chairs

But what if a pastor lacks the skill to chair an effective meeting? The first principle of meeting chairmanship is that the responsibility for chairing rests with the person who best runs a meeting. If the pastor cannot lead a session capably, the value of a well-run meeting stands higher than that of anyone leading it.

The pastor needs to honor that principle. He also needs to honor any effective, alternative meeting leadership.

Rotating chairmanship is ill-advised. Elected chairmanship is a not-at-all-worth-it shake-of-the-dice.

Since fill-in chairmanship ought to rest with the council member most competent, that qualification may need to be discerned. It may take some time and testing to do that.

A Clarification: What Does "Presiding" Mean?

Since canon law understands the pastor as presiding over each council, it is preferred that the pastor do so, even if he needs some support.

The Church's liturgy, however, clarifies that "presiding" can be understood from different perspectives. Whether dressed in vestments or sitting in choir robes on his throne, a bishop presides whenever he is present at the Sacred Liturgy, whichever way he exercises his role.

The bottom line is that the pastor "presides" if he is present, whether he chairs or not. Presiding fails the standard that absolutely requires the pastor to chair the meeting.

The Competent Chair

A particular constellation of skills in a chair will comfort meeting participants and build trust in the chair. The competent meeting chair:

LISTENS WELL...

* accurately summarizing,
* helping the group sort,
* clarifying ideas,
* focusing ideas into context, and
* writing contributions down.

INTEGRATES IDEAS...

* keeping the overarching context to the fore,
* relating ideas to one another,
* offering organizational options,
* asking provocative questions to further discussion,
* detaching from his or her point of view.

RESPECTS MEETING PARTICIPANTS...

* encouraging participation,
* honoring every participant,
* letting clarifying discussion run,
* bringing wandering discussion back to the point,
* landing the discussion at a meeting segment's end and a meeting's end, and
* landing the meeting with an effective summary, including the next steps.

Chairing is a Meeting Function, Not a Parish Office

Neither deference to the pastor's office, the desire for inclusivity, nor the honoring of personal popularity warrant derailing effectively run meetings. An effectively run meeting stands as a very high value for the councils. Consequently, the most capable and skilled person in the room ought to chair pastoral and finance council meetings.

Chairing council meetings is a matter of practical functioning for the group that is meeting. Council chairmanship is never a parish office.

DISCERNMENT DECISION-MAKING

DISCERNMENT DECISION-MAKING

Discerning Together

The Essential Synodality Practice

Implementing synodality practices calls parish leadership to discernment as the essential mode for decision-making. Why? Because honoring our common human dignity and exercising the co-responsibility we share as the baptized calls us to inclusive listening and dialogue. From that mutual exchange—consensus decision-making naturally flows, building life in the Holy Spirit and the Church's universal communion as the one body of Christ in a universal consensus in faith.

The Aim of Discernment

The Gospel call to shape pastoral ministry is the fundamental aim of all parish decision-making. That aim requires a process in which the decision-makers entrust themselves wholeheartedly to the gifts and power of the Holy Spirit, who animates the life of the Church and knows the way for us as a community of faith.

Parish ministry decision-making is neither solely the pastor's business nor the business of a particular leadership group or set of interest groups. Pastoral ministry decision-making remains always and essentially God's business.

Thus, the transforming method for communion-building decision-making in the parish is discernment: seeking together God's way for us as a community of faith.

A Spiritual Way

Discernment decision-making calls us to trust in the gifts and power of the Holy Spirit of God. Patient and reciprocal listening, prayerful dialogue and reflection, and surrender to whatever it is that God wants of us—these are the attitudes that ground discernment decision-making.

A Demanding Way

Discernment decision-making can be conflictual and arduous. It requires time and patience. New possibilities often arise, calling us in surprising directions. On the synodal path, discernment opens the parish beyond our vision to the Spirit's revelation and to the way of communion with one another and with God.

Discernment demands spiritual attitudes rooted in two questions we need to wrestle with in the decision-making process.

Question One: What Does God Want of Us?

The first and most fundamental question in discernment decision-making is this: what does God want of us?

On behalf of parish leadership and the whole assembly, discernment seeks God's will for the parish's Gospel ministry. Synodality practice places all parish decision-making, in every instance, under the wide umbrella of this penetrating-between-the-bone-and-the-marrow question.

The pastor's role in discernment is to keep the question—what does God want of us?—before the minds and hearts of council members, pastoral staff members, and the parish assembly.

The pastor exercises this role because the question connects the decision-making process to the Tradition and underlines the reality that the parish belongs to God and to the Church, not to the pastor or interest groups. The parish's vision, direction, and activity belong to God, the Church, and the whole parish community, not simply the pastor or the councils.

Parish decision-making, therefore, is grounded in prayer, not pastor-pleasing, whim, the best bargain, parishioner polls, people-pleasing, or even educated guesswork.

The whole process of decision-making for the

pastoral ministry of the parish is nothing less than sorting through the gifts and demands of the parish community's relationship with God.

Question Two: Can I Live With It?

Discernment decision-making always aims at unanimous decisions. Unanimity offers the best hope, practically and before God, of the rightness and peacefulness of decision.

Setting the bar at unanimity places a second question for participants in the discernment process: can I live with this decision? The answer to that question is the practical baseline for discernment decision-making. Not "Do I like it?" Not "Do I want it?" Rather, "Can I live with it?"

If a person cannot live with a decision made by the leadership group or community, that restless spirit raises fundamental questions about the advisability of the decision.

God abides deep within each human person, somewhere underneath our emotions and even below the depths of what we call "the gut." If a person cannot live with a decision, that fact needs to be made known, and the process needs to plunge deeper into the sorting—before God—until the way to unanimity is revealed.

If "What does God want of us?" is at the heart of the spiritual process of discernment and "Can I live with it?" is the practical baseline-before-God question for process participants, achieving unanimity among parish leaders and near unanimity in the parish assembly is nigh guaranteed.

Unanimity in the Parish Assembly

What precisely constitutes whole parish assembly consensus may itself need to be discerned.

For example, as roughly suggested by the rules of the German synodal way, actionable consensus may require 90% affirmation of the women gathered, 90% of the assembly gathered, and 100% of the parish pastoral leaders gathered—three separate votes.

While this kind of formula, which aims to right historical wrongs and give full voice to everyone, may be worthy of consideration, each parish needs to discern what constitutes consensus in its parish assembly.

In Pastoral Leadership Groups, Consensus Affirmation Needs to be Personally Registered

Fr. Roger laid before the finance council a delicate, touchy personnel matter that was highly controversial. After a lengthy discussion, he summarized the agreement he sensed. Then, briskly surveying the room, nodding heads confirmed a recommendation. Fr. Roger went with it.

When this issue broke out publicly in a parish assembly meeting, and with some heat, Fr. Roger told the assembly that the finance council unanimously agreed with his position.

A trustee stood up and publicly disagreed. Whatever the pastor thought he might have achieved by nodding heads did not constitute unanimous consensus in the trustee's mind. Though he said nothing in the meeting or to Fr. Roger afterward, he disagreed and had not nodded. This event undercut trust in Fr. Roger and halted the forward movement of his pastorate.

Consensus Decisions are Trustworthy

Particularly in parish leadership groups, when a consensus is reached, the pastor or process leader needs to ask each group member to speak out loud his or her "I can live with it" agreement. Why? Because once the group makes a decision, everyone in the group—including the pastor—must publicly stand with the consensus decision for the sake of the common good. That is, when group members leave a meeting where they have reached consensus, they go forth into the parish as ambassadors, not partisans. ∎

DISCERNMENT DECISION-MAKING

A Sample Discernment Process

A leadership group or assembly might follow several processes for discerning direction and action for a parish. Whatever mode of discernment is chosen, the process requires attitudes of faith, prayer, and freedom.

Grounded in Faith

Spiritual discernment requires that each person in the group be aware that God acts in my individual life and works with me in a unique way. That is, God's work in each person's life has particular and unique patterns, notes, and characteristics from which a person's holiness develops.

Discernment also requires that the group be aware that God works in groups and in a particular and unique way within each group. That is, each decision-making group has its own charisms and identity that focus energy.

Within discernment, awareness needs to be heightened so that the decision is made in an explicit atmosphere of faith that asks: what does God want of us?

Steeped in Prayer

Prayer nurtures sensitivity to those things that bring us close to God and inspire faith, hope, and love, as well as to those that distance us from God and result in faithlessness, hopelessness, and indifference.

Prayer also nurtures in us alertness to personal and corporate sinfulness and the dispositions that make us willing to face our weakness honestly.

Communion with God in prayer is the beginning, middle, and end of the discernment process. Discernment demands a heightened sense of our dependence on God, our need for naked honesty before God, and our call to surrender to God's will for us.

Reaching Out in Freedom

Freedom is the willingness to respond positively and constructively to whatever God may ask.

Freedom means remaining detached from the options that emerge in the decision-making process. Such freedom leads us to desire only pleasing God: wanting what God wants, receiving honor or scorn, riches or poverty, fame or anonymity, in whatever measure God wants it for us. The discernment process calls us to ask God for freedom from any hesitations or blocks in the decision-making process.

With these attitudes in place, nurtured in preparation for the process, the formal aspects of a discernment process begin.

Focus the Question

A discernment process starts with bringing the particular issue or concern into clear focus. That means first identifying the question to be considered.

This step requires study, research, evaluation, and sorting work to get to the facts of the situation. It also demands reviewing the group members' feelings and values relative to the issue or concern. In this step, the group strives to move toward the clarities of the moment while coming to a preliminary understanding and uncovering of the struggles within the group.

This step ignites learning to live with the discernment process and its outcome.

The results of this step should be a simple, declarative statement for the group's discernment.

Separate the Issues into Con and Pro

Next, the group looks at both sides of the issue or concern.

Begin with listing the cons. Cons are done first because they tend to disappear when done second. This step requires going around the circle repeatedly so each group member offers a con until all have spoken all of the cons they think relevant.

The same process is repeated for the pros. Equal time is given to both cons and pros.

The purpose of these steps is to uncover all the reasons—the real reasons—for the decision to be made.

Seek Areas of Common Agreement

Next, seek areas of agreement. Sometimes group members may not agree on the whole of a particular course of action, but articulating their agreement on elements of the issue may help them see more clearly what they do agree on and open up for everyone's view the direction consensus might take.

Reflect and Pray

If consensus is not readily achievable or a stalemate develops, time out for reflection and prayer can help the process. Perhaps the process needs to start again from the beginning. Perhaps the consensus might be that consensus is not possible. Perhaps people simply need time to reflect and pray.

The spaces in between sessions can be as integral to reaching consensus as reciprocal listening and discussion.

In such cases, the group might focus on their agreement and reach consensus about how to handle the issue for further consideration later. The group might also decide to drop the issue altogether.

In any case, the purpose of flexibly using prayer and reflection is to help achieve consensus.

Exterior and Interior Confirmation

After a decision is reached and before it is implemented, it needs to be monitored. If the decision is what God wants, the group should experience harmony. Interior confirmation is the experience of peace and joy in the Holy Spirit.

Exterior confirmation is the experienced congruency of the decision as it is announced and executed and the group's remaining appropriately detached from it.

Exterior confirmation includes the reality check of the decision's acceptance by the parish and legitimate authority and, even if it needs tweaking here and there, seeing it work out over time.

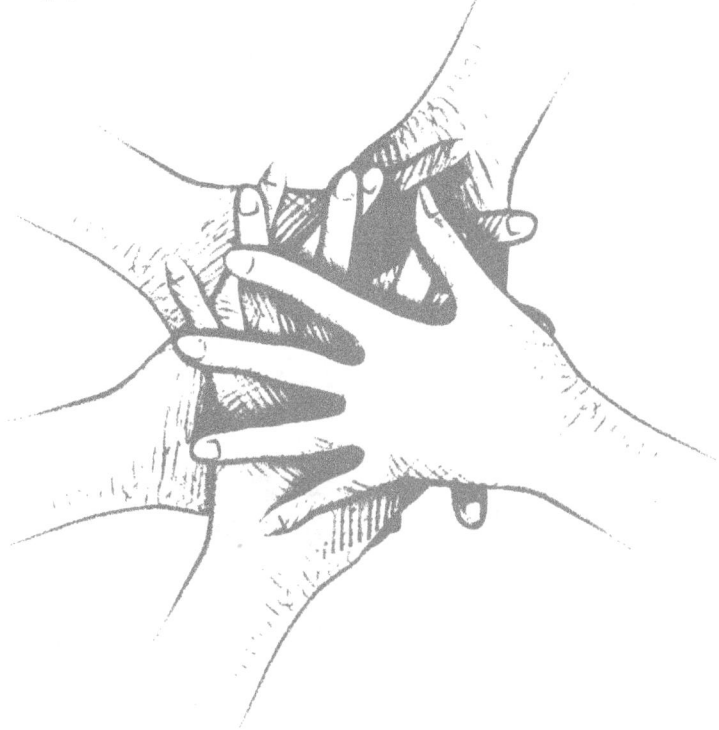

DISCERNMENT DECISION-MAKING

Further Reflections

When to Use a Formal Process

Very often, consensus in a parish leadership group is readily achievable without a formal discernment process.

As a rule of thumb, a full discernment process should be used with those issues which concern:

* the identity of the community,

* ministry expansion,

* staff expansion,

* a capital campaign,

* a facility building project,

* or issues in the community or a particular ministry that might be exceptionally volatile.

It Works: Two Examples

Discernment decision-making works. Two examples make the point. Both are factual experiences with university students.

In one university setting, 13 student leaders were responsible for placing hundreds of student volunteers in social service agencies near the university. The leadership group confronted this question: should student volunteers receive academic credit for their volunteer work?

In another university setting, in a nearly identical student volunteer program, 15 student leaders confronted this question: should student volunteers receive any form of compensation, even token compensation, for their volunteer work?

In both cases, the questions were perceived as central to the identity of the volunteer program. In each case, student leaders—a mix of men and women—had strong feelings, some on one side of the issue, some on the other. The discussions were heated. The group process took hours and included breaks for prayer and reflection. Tears flowed.

The discernment processes worked. One group unanimously decided to offer no academic credit to volunteers. The other chose to offer no compensation for student volunteering. Both leadership groups strongly affirmed that any form of material reward defied the purpose of the program for the university and the students participating.

Notably, in the first instance, the fierce conviction and persuasive power of one person eventually won the entire group over to her position. At the start of the process, all her peers disagreed with her.

In both instances, all group members were not only willing to live with the consensus decision but happy with it. Over time, the congruency of each decision was externally confirmed as well.

The Key Elements

The critical elements of the process that need to be kept in mind in discernment are three:

* the spiritual attitudes of faith, prayer, and freedom that ground consensus decision-making as a spiritual process;

* the question: what does God want of us?

* The question: can I live with this decision?

A most useful element of the process is the separating of the issue into cons first, then pros.

Voting

If all else breaks down and unanimous consensus seems impossible to achieve, would it make sense to take a vote and let the majority rule?

Many who have experienced such circumstances have found that the shift to voting, while painful, has ultimately worked out for two reasons:

* The great preponderance of the participants, over 90%, did achieve consensus.

✱ External affirmation changed minds and hearts as the decision-making body returned again and again to the basic decision and its implementation.

If a decision is right for a community, even those who have held back from consensus around the original decision may very well agree eventually.

But moving to a vote is a high-risk strategy in an assembly of synodal practice because voting may undercut communion in the long run and shortcut the Holy Spirit's course, more certainly affirmed in consensus. ■

THE MINISTRY STAFF

THE MINISTRY STAFF
Staff Titles

The Meaning of a Title

A job title names a role given within an organization. A title combines keywords that describe both job responsibilities and the holder's level of experience. Job titles are deliberate and formal. A title always points to a position description, a listing of general and specific performance responsibilities.

A title also properly discloses something of the identity and purpose of the entity within which the title holder exercises his or her responsibilities and, by implication, all other entities like it.

Transitional Pressure

Starting in the late 1960s, the burgeoning rise of lay staff members demanded that the Church create titles for new parish and diocesan positions in liturgy, religious education, pastoral care, administration, and outreach. During this transition, perhaps just by luck, faith communities looked to the business corporation for staff titles. The notable titles implemented on parish and diocesan staff during this time were those beginning with "director" and "coordinator." "Business administrator" would be included in this movement.

The Choices We Made

This title implementation, with the added phrase "of religious education," "of pastoral care," or "of parish outreach," etc., has served us in a practical way for more than half a century. Parishioners know what a liturgy director does and understand spontaneously that an RE coordinator does less than an RE director.

Well and simply done… we thought!

Two Noteworthy Inklings of Contradictions

Two ensuing movements exposed the awkwardness the Church let in the door by reaching into the corporate paradigm.

First, pastors commonly presumed that if they are the *employer*—the staff supervising agent for the parish—and staff members are *employees*—the subjects of the employer's exercise of authority—then the pastor is an "at will" employer free to hire and fire whomever he chooses, whenever he chooses, as he chooses.

This naive but very real presupposition still causes parishes, dioceses, and staff members serious problems. Not the least of the difficulties is the clash between the clerical culture's semi-monarchical authority assumptions and both legal employment reality and parish politics… never mind the conflicts this mentality creates in relation to the Gospel!

Second, the problems compelled dioceses to engage human resources professionals, some of whom became diocesan staff members, to draw up and enforce employment guidelines and to coach pastors and others about what is required for establishing and advertising a job as well as interviewing, hiring, supervising, evaluating, disciplining, and terminating staff members.

Human resources personnel offer the Church essential professional services in the struggle to order employment relationships properly. More about that later. At the same time, however, human resources professionals help solve only some problems some of the time. Why? The clerical culture's stout authority assumptions are entrenched, and they grow more strident the higher one goes in Church hierarchy. Consequently, human resources professionals are sometimes confined to offering the Church angles for smoothing over problems rather than enforceable yet gracious processes for happy employment, heading problems off, or eliminating them.

Moreover, establishing human resources personnel in dioceses has pulled the Church deeper into the corporate paradigm and the hands of lawyers.

A Provocative Third Inkling

A third movement during recent decades even more clearly reveals the Church's ill fit with the corporate business paradigm.

To preserve the pastor's ministerial role and offer a shield against weighing a pastor down with "administration," a position arose in parishes that gathered staff supervision and other administrative oversight responsibilities into a single job.

In some settings, the title for this position evokes the corporate business paradigm: "parish administrator." This title, while understandable, is problematic. It can easily be confused with the position "business administrator," which is sometimes a supervisory position but most often assumes responsibility for money and property. Second, the title risks canonical confusion. In canon law, a person assigned a pastor's responsibilities but neither unlimited tenure nor a specified term of office—often a priest—is designated the parish "administrator." This "pastor lite," canonically defined position and titling, aims to offer the bishop appointment flexibility, not create confusion.

A more provocative titling for this "administration" position used in some settings is "pastoral associate." This title follows more closely a church and relational paradigm, suggesting that the position remains closely connected with the pastor, shares elements of pastor authority, and supervises ministry. "Pastoral associate" also carries with it the whiff of what used to be called the "associate pastor" position, one often held by the second parish priest after the pastor when parish clergy were abundant.

Still, the bare title "pastoral associate" is soft and misses the mark. It offers little indication of the job's responsibilities or the holder's level of experience.

A Proposed Resolution

The title usage that follows here rests on this conviction: our parish and diocesan position titles ought always to evoke *first* the ministry and relationship mission of the Church, and then clearly designate the job's responsibilities.

Consequently, for staff positions that share in shepherding ministry, roles delegated major ministerial oversight, the title begins: "pastoral associate."

This designation implies a full-time staff member. The delegation of the shepherding ministry oversight relationship and responsibility, however, remains the essential point, not the time frame.

Second, because major oversight ministries have a designated area of responsibility, the title includes "for…" and the specific area. Thus, in what follows, the DRE is titled "pastoral associate for religious education," the diocesan liturgy director is titled "bishop's pastoral associate for worship," the business administrator is titled "pastoral associate for business affairs," the principal is titled "pastoral associate for education."

This proposed practice aims to explicitly connect staff positions to a relationship with the shepherding ministry of the pastor or bishop and thus to the mission of the Church, even as it aims to do clearly what a job title is supposed to do.

Synodality Provokes Us to Rethink

Communion in mission as Church means that on every level of co-responsibility and accountability, we are about not merely performative roles, tasks, and functions but Gospel ministry. That is, through the gifts and power of the Holy Spirit, all the Church and all its ministers aim first for personal encounter in listening and dialogue: building relationship with Jesus Christ and one another, as we share the Word in all we do, follow the pattern of life Jesus taught us, and are sent forth in mission to the relational transformation of the world. ■

THE MINISTRY STAFF
Decision-Making

The Parish's Pastoral Staff

The pastor serves as a ministry generalist who oversees, enables, and monitors all parish ministry. The pastor strives to build consensus around the parish's vision and support the other pastoral leaders of the parish, and the parish as a whole, so all are set free to exercise their co-responsible ministry.

In a collegial relationship with the pastor, pastoral staff members—ordinarily professionals educated in a ministry field—oversee and resource the implementation of a parish's Gospel ministry, supervise other ministers, and set and monitor a budget area.

Co-Pastors of the Parish

The members of the pastoral staff serve as co-pastors of the parish. The term *co-pastor*—a bold term that raises hackles in some circles, but that is accurate nonetheless—points to a double level of collegial relationship with the pastor: individual and group.

Collegial Relationship with the Pastor

A pastoral staff member, in a collegial relationship with the pastor, holds broad discretionary oversight responsibility for the ministry area in his or her portfolio, everything from the ministry's vision to its implementation particulars. The parish hires a pastoral staff member for this purpose.

A pastoral staff member complements the pastor's generalist stance by approaching the parish's life through the prism of his or her portfolio. This approach nuances individual and group perspectives during listening and dialogue. The focused perspective of a pastoral staff member gives fuller shape to the pastor's, pastoral staff's, leadership group's, and parish's ministry vision.

The pastoral associate for worship, for example, views the parish from the angle of the treasury of the Church's liturgical and musical tradition and invites the pastor, fellow staff members, and the parish to be mindful of that perspective, which stretches everyone's understanding of the parish and its ministry. The pastoral associate for catechesis does the same from the perspective of the church's catechetical tradition.

The contribution a pastoral associate makes to the parish and pastoral leadership from his or her ministry perch provides wonderful color, texture, breadth, and depth to everything the parish plans and does.

In turn, the history and culture of the parish, the pastor, colleagues, parishioners, and the council-established vision for the parish all have their effect on the pastoral associate's ministry-focused stance as they shape the contribution the pastoral associate makes to parish life.

The Pastoral Staff as a College

Each pastoral associate, sometimes called a *director*, is also a member of the little college called the pastoral staff, which gathers regularly with the pastor. The pastoral staff, pastor, and pastoral associates together form "the pastoring ministry" of the parish.

That is, the pastoring ministry of the parish is complete only in the context of the whole pastoral ministry collegial group, pastor and pastoral staff members together.

Each pastoral staff member represents an aspect or element of the whole in accord with his or her ministry portfolio.

Even the pastor, though a generalist, represents essentially the presidential ministry of the parish. The pastor cannot represent the fullness of the parish's worship or religious education ministry, nor does the pastor represent the totality of the parish's ministries. A parishioner's questions about religious education classes or choir membership, for instance, require the pastor to forward them to a pastoral associate.

The whole pastoral staff gathered together as a group expresses the fullness of "pastor" and "Gospel ministry" for the parish community.

A Most Welcome Affirmation

Several months after beginning his pastorate and after listening, dialogue, and developing mutual understanding with the pastoral staff, Fr. Bertrand announced to the parish assembly:

"I want everyone to understand that the pastoral staff members (he named them) are, with me, co-pastors of the parish. Each of us has a necessary role, and we all constitute what it is to pastor this community. So, when any pastoral staff member is in the room, the eyes and ears of the pastoring ministry of the parish are in the room. Please honor their role. They are good at what they do. Please bring forward to any of them your needs and concerns. They will respond as best they can. Please support them in their ministry. They exercise ministry with me for the sake of the whole parish community."

The announcement raised eyebrows in the parish assembly. As the weeks and months passed, however, the pastoral staff members grew more confident and relaxed in their roles, more trusting of the pastor and one another, and more collaborative in their ministry exercise. Parishioners grew more respectful toward the pastoral staff members personally and the contributions to parish life the staff members offered. The announcement and the follow-through from pastor and staff built personal relationships, communion in ministry, and trust in the community.

The Church, the Parish, and the Pastoral Staff

Part of the pastoral staff's role for the community of faith is to reflect together regularly with the pastor on the parish's Gospel ministry.

This reflection takes place in a very full ecclesial context for the pastoral minister:

* the ministry guidelines promulgated by the universal, national, and local church;
* the limits and possibilities articulated by the diocese and the pastor;
* the vision for the parish set by the pastoral council;
* the allocation of resources established by the finance council; and
* the sensibilities developed by the commission which assist the pastoral staff member in his or her area of ministry.

Pastoral Staff on the Synodal Way

Pastoring the parish, in general, and from every angle, is the collegial purpose of the pastoral staff, the pastor presiding over the college's ministry as each member fulfills his or her particular and complementary role within the parish community.

Consequently, pastoral staff member participation in the discernment processes that shape the parish's identity and mission is a critical mandate for the pastor, parish pastoral leadership, the parish assembly, and the pastoral staff member.

The structure of that participation may vary. In most instances, collegial participation would be most pleasant. Occasionally, pastoral staff members may lead this or that discernment process. In other cases, a staff member may participate as one among many in the parish.

However, participation is structured, full pastoral staff participation in listening, dialogue, deciding, implementing, and evaluating the parish's ministry direction and commitment is integral to an effective implementation of synodal practices in the parish. ∎

THE MINISTRY STAFF
Communion in Co-Pastoring

The Arena of Pastoral Staff as Co-Pastors

Implementation of this vision requires three levels of meetings for the pastoral associate:

* the one-to-one meeting with the pastor,
* the pastoral staff group meeting,
* and the meeting with the pastoral staff member's ministry area parishioner-staffed commission.

The effective pastoral associate will conscientiously participate regularly in all these meeting levels and strive in their listening, dialoguing, discerning, decision-making, and decision-taking to be as participative, constructive, forthright, accountable, and forward-looking as possible.

The One-on-One with the Pastor

Whether they are full-time or part-time, paid or volunteer, and whatever the blend of their ministry responsibilities, a pastoral associate and pastor need a regular, one-to-one meeting. This meeting's aim:

* to develop common expectations for ministry,
* to learn the strengths and weaknesses of the parish's ministry landscape,
* to clarify performance concerns,
* offer perspective on performance weaknesses,
* to elicit reasons for falling short of expectations,
* to open planning possibilities,
* and to deepen the relationship between the pastor and pastoral associate.

So long as this meeting is a reciprocal give-and-take process between the pastor and pastoral associate, it will help develop competencies, clarify expectations, strengthen bonds, nurture mutual understanding, and build trust.

The meeting can also be a great deal of fun as the pastor and pastoral associate explore mutually interesting theological issues, practical concerns, and pastoral approaches to individuals and groups.

While formal individual meetings need absolutely to occur at least twice per year for supervisory purposes, informal, casual meetings circulating about the parish center and popping into one another's office help to build easy rapport among pastor and staff.

While the frequency and formality of the meeting might be determined by the size of the parish more than any other single factor, as a rule of thumb, the pastor and pastoral associate hold an individual meeting about every other week, twice a month.

The Pastoral Staff Group Meeting

The group meeting has a distinct purpose for the pastoral associates and pastor. This meeting's aim:

* to tie back and tie across basic information about each of the ministries and the whole parish,
* to help the pastoral associates and pastor together clarify a common vision for the parish,
* to encourage the members of the group to become increasingly collaborative in their ministry together,
* to share resources,
* and to build group relationships.

Variations by Example

Because the shape of these meetings varies from parish to parish, some examples may help set some boundaries.

KEEP STAFF FUNCTIONS FOCUSED

When St. Lawrence holds its staff meeting, everyone comes: the pastor, pastoral staff, secretaries, and the maintenance supervisor.

While this sort of meeting may be useful occasionally for sharing information, it inhibits pastoral staff discussion and planning for Gospel ministry while it risks engaging secondary and distracting concerns. It also can pull administrative staff members into pastoral staff concerns, which can be confusing and even disruptive for the meeting, staff relationships, and good order for parish ministry.

The pastoral staff holds the Gospel ministry portfolio in all its depth and complexity. Other staff groups exercise different responsibilities. Each group needs to be honored in its own sphere with separate meetings so that effective, focused Gospel ministry might move forward.

KEEP MINISTRY FOCUSED

St. Simeon's staff meetings bog down in pastoral staff members' personal relationship concerns and activity planning.

Because staff members seek the satisfaction of their personal needs in their professional relationships, hidden agendas create rumblings that keep them from constructive parish ministry business. Planning activities and lunches out—gracious as these can be on occasion—can also distract the staff.

Ministry requires focus. While an occasional luncheon or outing has its place, that place is secondary to staff meetings. Staff members must also be encouraged to seek counsel and friendship outside the workplace.

RESOLVE STAFF CONFLICT

The staff at St. Olaf dislike each other. Ideological divergence, turf battles, and personality differences—the bowling balls under the table—make the parish office and staff meetings tense.

This situation requires strong, creative leadership that calls staff members to professional attitudes and polite cooperation that rises above disagreement and disaffection so the staff can plan and collaborate. This kind of stress may call for occasional blunt talk at a meeting to set boundaries. An incisive pastor may conclude that staff change is the only remedy.

Communion in Ministry is the Aim

The pastor and pastoral associates benefit greatly in their ministry together if they do the hard work of cohering the pastoral staff in their ministry as professionals, ministers, and co-pastors who share oversight of the whole parish assembly and its Gospel ministry life.

The pastoral staff's communion in ministry ignites, supports, and informs its collaboration with parishioners in pastoral ministry commissions.

THE MINISTRY STAFF

Commissions & Decision-Making

The Ministry Commission

The third meeting context for pastoral staff ministry—beyond meeting with the pastor one-to-one and the pastoral staff group meeting—is the ministry commission. Each Gospel ministry of the parish or ministries blend overseen by a pastoral associate, requires a commission.

Pastoral staff members come and go. The parishioners are stable; they remain. It is a high value, therefore, that parishioners participate in focusing, directing, and monitoring each of the parish's ministries, just as they do in council for the whole parish's ministry. Ministry commissions offer continuity, help keep ministry organically centered in the parishioner experience, and widen the parishioners' knowledge base about the parish's ministry.

Leadership Group Designations

* **Council** – a group called together for consultation, discussion, and advice.

* **Commission** – a group called together to perform specified duties.

* **Committee** – a group appointed to investigate or report on select matters. This task-oriented group is always *ad hoc*.

* **Board** – persons who gather to manage or control an entity continuously. Parishes have none but a corporate board.

Commission members offer an irreplaceable complement to the pastoral associate because of the depth and breadth of their experience of and access to fellow parishioners day-to-day. Commissions also spread ministry knowledge and experience across the parish, enriching parish life.

Commission membership serves as a major formational tool for the parish, and the commission nurtures the bonds of communion among parishioners, even as they shape pastoral leadership.

The Commission's Function

The ministry commission's purpose is to focus, guide, and monitor a particular Gospel ministry in a collaborative relationship with the pastoral associate. That mission parallels that of the pastoral council in relationship with the pastor.

The ministry commission:

* assists with planning for the Gospel ministry area,

* offers recommendations on ministry direction concerns brought before the pastoral council,

* reviews the ministry area budget before it goes to the finance council,

* and advises the pastoral associate on all matters he or she brings before it.

* If necessary, the commission establishes *ad hoc* committees to assist it with its work.

The Commission and Planning

Planning for a particular ministry area is the backbone of the commission's work. Effective planning by a commission requires the pastoral associate to educate the commission members about the ministry area: its purpose and history, the universal and national church guidelines that govern its mission, the various pastoral considerations that determine this or that course of action, its financial demands on and benefit to the parish, and its relationship to the other Gospel ministries.

The pastoral associate's priority needs to be thoroughly equipping the commission members for their ministry so they will offer effective pastoral leadership. This education and formation will look different for each ministry area.

Decision-Making

Commission decision-making relies on the same discernment process as the councils and the parish assembly and is therefore governed by the same two questions: What does God want of us? Can I live with this decision? Spirituality grounds the process, and a formal, spiritually-based discernment process backs the commission's effort to achieve unanimity in its decisions.

Structuring Commissions

Structuring a ministry commission's task requires careful attention. The province of the commission should be the large overview:

* the ministry's general contours and direction in the parish,
* ministry area policy,
* and concerns the pastoral associate finds it helpful to discuss with the commission.

Because each Gospel ministry demands expertise to implement it, the day-to-day details of Gospel ministry should be left to the pastoral associate.

For Example: A Worship Commission

Isaiah Pope, the pastoral associate for worship, established a worship commission at St. Cajetan's. It took four meetings for the parishioners to tell their personal stories and get acquainted with their basic responsibilities, two meetings for Isaiah to offer a basic overview of the Church's liturgy and introduce the commission members to the liturgical books, and ten meetings for Isaiah and the commission members to read and reflect together on the topics that fundamentally educated its members for the commission's work: the Church, the sacraments, the range of liturgical rites, and pastoral liturgy, for example, why celebrate the Liturgy of the Hours instead of a communion service on weekdays, or why bring the body for the funeral rather than cremated remains, or why do we insist on witnessing marriages in church instead of on the beach.

This first year of education readied the commission members ably so they could help Isaiah over the next two years to shape a pastoral liturgy that belonged to St. Cajetan's, formulate policy in the liturgy area, evaluate liturgical celebrations and seasons, and equip incoming commission members—all the while minimizing the commission's temptation to micromanage, which every pastoral leadership group will do if given the chance.

If a commission can be effectively structured for liturgy, it can be effectively structured for any ministry area!

Commission Benefits

Participation in commissions:

* educates parishioners about the basics of Gospel ministry;
* honors parishioners' rightful place in focusing, guiding, and monitoring the parish's ministries;
* places parishioners at every level of ministry planning and discernment;
* offers continuity and insight within and across the parish's Gospel ministries;
* builds parish community life;
* centers the pastoral associate in real parishioner experience of ministry;
* and prepares parishioners to serve in parish and diocesan governance structures.

Formed in the Synodal Way

The parish ministry commission is an indispensable tool for forming people in the practices of the synodal way. Commission experience also builds and transforms the community over time, moving it forward toward the deep evangelization that our age requires. ∎

THE MINISTRY STAFF
Administrative Staff

Who Are They?

All parishes have administrative staff members: administrative assistants, receptionists, bookkeepers, kitchen coordinators, and maintenance personnel. These staff members collaborate with the pastor and pastoral staff, providing support for the Gospel ministries of the parish mainly in the following areas:

* communications & technology,
* finances,
* property management,
* hospitality,
* and record keeping.

In larger parish settings, administrative staff members serve in a complementary, supportive relationship not only with the pastor but also with individual pastoral staff members in their area of ministry.

The Communication Context

Pastoral and administrative staff collaboration requires regular and clear communication. Informing the receptionist about an expected guest or the procedure for announcing a guest, providing useful and timely information for the bulletin and website, tracking how much money is left in the budget and how much to budget for next year, adhering faithfully to the room reservation procedures, forwarding information for baptismal certificate recording—all of these tasks, and far more, require close collaboration between pastoral and administrative staff members.

Job performance communication and collaboration with administrative staff members best occurs in individual rather than in group settings.

Formal Communication Boundaries

Formal feedback and clarification interviews between an administrative staff member and his or her supervisor need to occur twice per year. The emphasis of a supervisor's meeting with an administrative staff member would include:

* developing common expectations,
* problem-solving
* clarifying performance concerns, and
* deepening communion in relationship.

Informal, casual communications and clarifications usually fill the bill day-to-day between a supervisor and administrative staff member.

Occasionally, procedure establishment and policy change involve an administrative staff member in a pastoral staff meeting. This collaboration, natural and necessary, is best kept focused and time-limited.

Performance concerns, should they arise, belong between a supervisor and the staff member. Conversation among other staff members about such matters, other than functional fact-finding, is inappropriate.

Their Critical Contribution

Administrative staff members offer a singular and valuable perspective on the parish's Gospel ministry because of their unique positions. A secretary knows who comes and goes, who calls whom, and often hears opinions and evaluations unavailable to anyone else. A maintenance man or kitchen coordinator offers a gritty perspective on who gets along with whom, fundamental relationship prejudices, and which people or group controls what is in the facilities. Administrative staff members often experience the informal power centers in the parish much more immediately and accurately than the pastoral staff or pastor.

Administrative staff members typically know who is well-served by the parish and who is not because of their immediacy to ministry service.

Administrative staff also understand the depth, breadth, and complexity of the parish's infrastructure strengths and weaknesses far better than the pastor or pastoral staff because of their day-to-day engagement.

Administrative staff participation in pastoral ministry decision-making, therefore, typically offers granular data helpful for making well-informed and balanced decisions.

At the same time, participation in the ordinary pastoral staff meeting, unless an agenda item focuses on their immediate expertise, dribbles away valuable time for administrative staff members.

Structuring Participation

Consequently, administrative staff participation in major pastoral decision-making for the parish needs to be solidly in place but judiciously framed.

Participation might be structured in several ways. In some cases, administrative staff participation with the pastor and pastoral staff offers a more complete perspective. That sharing in the group is best sought and appropriately structured. In other cases, gathering the administrative staff only, with a agreeable and safe meeting chair, can free them up for free exchange and fuller participation in parish direction. In other cases, administrative staff participation individually in this or that parishioner grouping can facilitate comfortable and effective involvement in discernment decision-making.

Precise need in each circumstance best determines how administrative staff contributions are best structured.

At the Center, Not on the Periphery

Whatever form administrative staff participation might take, the pastor, pastoral staff, and parish leadership need to remain aware that, though they are often unsung and taken for granted, parish administrative staff members offer singular, valuable, and even critical perspectives to discernment decision-making.

Many a parish would descend into chaos and wrangling without the effective ministry of administrative staff members. Their point-of-view is essential to complete decision-making and synodal practice. ∎

PARISHES WITH SCHOOLS

PARISHES WITH SCHOOLS

School As Parish Ministry

Creative Tension

In 2023, there were 5,935 parish schools across the United States. A parochial school graces and strains a parish community. Some parishes support the school vigorously, while others feel ambivalent. In either case, many tout the school as the parish's central mission.

While educating and forming children is at least as much of a gift to a parish as it is a responsibility, the tendency to supersize the school's importance, fog its purpose, isolate it from the rest of the parish, and see it as competing for parish resources can create stress for parishes with schools. A balanced perspective on a school's proper place challenges every parish with a school.

Three areas deserve particular attention:

* the tendency to see the school as a separate institution instead of a parish ministry,

* the proper relationship balance between the principal and the pastor and pastoral staff, and

* the governance structure that best serves the parish and the school.

Not a Separate Institution But a Parish Ministry

Most parishioners and pastoral leaders, as well as parents with children in the school, tend to treat a school as an entity independent of the parish. This sense of separation begins with language that refers to "the school" and to "the parish" or "the church." It is reinforced in many ways:

* A physically separate school building/address.

* The high visibility and regimented calendar of a school ministry—175 days of children, parents, patrols, visiting teams, and traffic.

* The focused intensity of parents for their children and the commonality families share.

* The disconnect between families' school commitment and parish commitment—participating faithfully in school activities but haphazardly in Sunday Mass and stewardship

Further, teaching staff tend to be understandably bonded and hold themselves apart from the rest of the parish staff. They sometimes give loyalty to the principal over and against the pastor. Teachers are often ambivalent about their faith and often not parishioners (certainly more so than the women religious teachers of the past).

Most pastoral leaders acquiesce to this sense of separation because it seems natural. Accepting it, however, serves as a contrary sign within the parish and to the world.

The School: Parish Ministry

A school is one among all the parish's ministries.

The fundamental justification for a parish school is its forming children in faith. That was the parochial school's original purpose beginning in the 1850s. As immigrants arrived on our shores, parish schools multiplied—mandated in the 1880s—so that the Church might educate newcomers to thrive in American culture, yes, but primarily to form future generations for participation in the Catholic Church.

This purpose remains the same today: forming children in worship, Catholic Tradition, spirituality, service to others, living and valuing community, charitable work, and social justice principles and action. These are the parish's Gospel-based ministry to its school children. A community of faith owes its children this ministry.

St. John School Ministry

When Fr. Frank became pastor of St. John the Baptist, he saw immediately the school's strong sense of separation from the parish. He heard the ordinary language indicating that but also read in

THE LISTENING PARISH

the school's PR materials that the school was private and Christian, not parochial and Catholic. The principal told him she expected little connection with Fr. Frank. The school board sets tuition, staff salaries, and budget. Competition for parish financial resources was fierce. Parents often put the principal on the spot about day-to-day school matters at school board meetings.

Firm that school was a parish ministry, Fr. Frank began to talk about that. He won over the principal largely by protecting her from being put on the spot in school board meetings. When the middle school religion teacher retired, the pastoral associate for religious formation consented to teach middle school religion with an eye to winning over the faculty enough to reshape the elementary and intermediate religion curriculum. The pastoral associate for worship consented to teach a middle school liturgical music and history session each week.

Offering a money-saving rationale, Fr. Frank gradually took all bookkeeping, technology assistance, and public relations services for the parish's ministries into the parish's main office. He modified the school board's place in the budget process by asserting that, while the board needed to offer input, it was the role of the finance and pastoral councils to approve the parish budget, and that included the school.

Eventually, as the pastor, principal, pastoral staff, and other pastoral leaders reflected and conferred, they decided to implement a language shift. They began to call the school "the school ministry." They modified the street signs that said "Nativity of John the Baptist School" and "Nativity of John the Baptist Church" to say simply "Nativity of John the Baptist." Since it served the religious education program and the school ministry, the staff began referring to "the classroom building" instead of "the school." After they moved the parish offices into the building, they began to refer to it as "the ministry center" and had that name placed above the main entry. After some years, the school board voted itself out of existence and voted in a school ministry commission to replace it.

These changes, done gradually over eight years, won attention. Staff and parishioners talked and asked about them. Despite occasional irritable exchanges expressing fears that the school was losing importance, two pastors after Fr. Frank, the changes remained. Nativity of John the Baptist grew ever more deeply into the understanding that the school is a ministry of the parish, not a separate institution.

Embracing School Ministry

On the synodal way, pastoral leaders would do well to structure language, staff relationships, and governance structures to clarify that the school is a ministry. Parishes with schools need to proclaim in word and act, and on every level of their life that the school is not a separate institution but a parish ministry.

The Notes of a Parish School Ministry's Catholic Identity

- Regular Mass and worship.
- A Catholic administrator.
- Mostly practicing Catholics on the faculty.
- Parish council oversight of governance policies and finances.
- Parent participation in governance and policymaking.
- Non-shaming and formational discipline.
- Differentiated instruction.
- Parish pastoral associates engaged in teaching religious studies, liturgy, and service.
- A carefully structured and focused religion curriculum.
- Sacramental preparation integrated with the whole parish.
- Commitment to community service.
- Religious art throughout the environment.
- A spirit of quiet and order.
- School building use for other parish ministries.

PARISHES WITH SCHOOLS

The School Principal

The Principal: Not a Lone Wolf

The relationship between the pastor, the pastoral staff, and the school principal has an enormous impact on integrating the school into the Gospel ministry life of the parish and vice versa. Consequently, the structure of these relationships requires particular and careful consideration.

Principal: A Problematic Title

The title principal, with its strong disciplinary undertones in education culture, suggests that the position's occupant enjoys a kind of independence that a principal simply does not have in a parish school ministry.

Carrying out the education culture logic of the title principal within a parochial school setting would demand this understanding: if the head of the school ministry is the principal, then the pastor is the parish school ministry's superintendent. While this language clarifies roles, it stands practically unworkable in a parish context.

The Principal: A Pastoral Associate

In a parish setting, the principal might most accurately be titled *pastoral associate for education/principal*.

This nomenclature acknowledges the position's proper place in both parish culture and education culture.

Pointing to the principal's immediate relationship with the pastor, intimate connection with the pastoring ministry, and collegial relationship with the other pastoral associates, the title *pastoral associate for education/principal* accurately mirrors the placeholder's relational context and priorities in the parish.

Retaining the title *principal* gives an appropriate nod to education culture and the real authority the position has in a school. At the same time, the whole title affirms that, in a parish setting, the principal as pastoral associate role serves the essential priorities and values of the parish. This title clarity helps the principal, the teaching staff, parents with children in the school, the parish's pastoral leadership, and the parishioners at large.

Roles and Collegial Relationship

The pastoral associate for education/principal, however, holds a unique position among the parish's pastoral leaders.

Unlike other pastoral associates, a principal typically supervises from 11 to 40 people or more, manages a seven-figure budget, supervises the arrangement and maintenance of 30,000 square feet of space, serves a large and passionately interested constituency, and is entrusted with the security and future of the parish's children for seven hours a day, 175 days a year. The principal, therefore, has considerable authority and power and needs to build on that through his or her educational leadership.

Moreover, if the pastor is the generalist on the ministry staff for the parish, the pastoral associate/principal serves as a generalist on the school ministry staff for that ministry.

At the same time, the principal serves as a specialist: the educator's educator, the disciplinarian's disciplinarian, and the employment supervisor of a large staff.

The Pastor and the Principal

The magnitude of the principal's responsibility and the context of the office's exercise demand that the pastor and principal collaborate in a particularly sensitive way. The wise and collegial pastor will acknowledge, respect, and honor the principal's leadership role and hard-won expertise.

At the same time, the pastor oversees the whole parish's Gospel mission and its vision. That includes the school ministry along with the ministries of the other pastoral associates. The pastor remains accountable to the bishop, the councils, and the parish for all matters of law, property, personnel, and finances in the parish, which includes the school ministry. The pastor also supervises the pastoral associate for education/principal. Consequently, the wise pastoral associate for education/principal works in a closely cooperative relationship with the pastor day-to-day, takes the pastor's cues seriously, strives for a common vision, and accepts coaching on the areas of the pastor's inalienable responsibilities. Not doing so can wreak havoc in a parish and pull the rug out from under the pastor and pastoral associate's relationship.

Collegial Relationship: An Example

Mr. Taylor Dennehy was pastoral associate for education/principal of a 257-student parish school ministry in a city neighborhood. One Thursday during lunch, a student reported lipstick writing on the boys' bathroom mirror. When Mr. Dennehy checked it out, the writing threatened the use of a gun. He immediately informed the police, left a message for the pastor, talked with the middle school faculty about restricting student activity, and began investigative work that narrowed the writing down to a small group of 8th-grade boys. When the pastor called at 2:30, Mr. Dennehy told him the police had not come, the boys refused to name names, and the teachers were restless. The pastor could tell that Mr. Dennehy was exhausted and discombobulated. He offered to help.

The pastor went to Mr. Dennehy's office and outlined a plan for the rest of the day: a letter to all parents explaining the incident and what was done to handle it, an approach to the 8th-grade boys through their parents, a brief end-of-the-day faculty meeting for information-sharing and preparation for the next morning, and a parent-led body-search process for middle schoolers the following morning to offer parents assurances in case the culprit was not yet named. Admitting his being beside himself, Mr. Dennehy agreed to the plan and plunged in. The pastor crafted the parent letter for Mr. Dennehy's signature, then left him to follow through on the plan, with occasional phone calls to check-in.

In the weeks afterward, the culprit caught, teachers calm, and the parent community satisfied, Mr. Dennehy won kudos for handling the situation. For his part, the pastor felt deeply content that, in the breach, he had Mr. Dennehy's thanks and had helped preserve his power.

Serving the Parish's Mission

If the pastoral associate for education/principal serves the mission of the parish as articulated by the councils and led by the pastor; takes the pastor's coaching regarding law, personnel, property, and finances; and ministers in a collegial relationship with the other pastoral associates; then he or she will shine in the parish like a new penny.

If the pastor respects and honors the pastoral associate for education/principal's expertise, coaches gently and sagaciously, backs up the pastoral associate consistently, and trusts him or her, then the pastor serves well the pastoral associate, the school ministry, and the parish.

The Dance is a Delicate One

The relationship between a pastoral associate/principal and pastor demands close communication, keen mutual respect, kind forthrightness, a deep humility that gives the other the benefit of the doubt, and an alert preserving of trust. Why? With far more intensity than with other pastoral associates and their ministries, when the monarch and the duke contend, civil war is the ever-threatening and unhappy result. ∎

PARISHES WITH SCHOOLS

School Ministry Governance

School Board: A Problematic Term

In the U.S., a public school board is a legal entity whose authority is based on the independent incorporation of the schools under its jurisdiction. A board's role is to provide direction and oversight to an educational institution.

Unless a school is independently incorporated—true for many high and elementary schools that belong to clustered parishes but not for most parish schools—the term school board is a misnomer in a parish context.

The term *school board* sets up parents and board members with misleading expectations and contrary presuppositions. These inevitably bring it into conflict with the pastor and councils.

Worse, a board sometimes sets itself against the pastoral associate for education/principal because its members ask questions without boundaries that hold the pastoral associate/principal publicly accountable for relatively trivial matters, which usually and rightfully belong to the pastoral associate for education/principal's office or within his or her relationship with the pastor.

Organic Communion with the Parish

For the sake of the consistent and organic growth in communion of the parish and its constituent ministries, school governance concerns are most appropriately and effectively handled by the parish's ordinary leadership structures: collegial relationship with the pastor and pastoral staff, the pastoral council, the finance council, and a school ministry commission.

The School Ministry and the Parish's Councils

A parish's school ministry is cared for most properly in the same way and with the same leadership structures as the other parish ministries.

That is, the parish's pastoral council oversees the school's long-range planning, evaluates it as a ministry of the parish, and monitors and makes recommendations about its financial, legal, property, and personnel aspirations and developments. The parish's finance council sets tuition, recommends staff raises or freezes according to those recommended for the parish staff, establishes a budget, consults with the pastor and pastoral associate about personnel and legal issues, and monitors the school ministry's building and maintenance. Both bodies see that the school ministry's personnel policies, legal practices, and fundraising policies cohere with those of the rest of the parish's ministries.

Mindful of the financial proportion of the school ministry in a parish budget and the large number of persons affected by it, a school ministry still most properly receives the same focus, guidance, and monitoring by the councils as do all the other ministries of the parish.

Respecting Communion Can Be Hard

Fr. Martin went on sabbatical. Before he left, he worked closely with the pastoral associate for education/principal and both councils to establish the school ministry budget for the next year—tuition, salary raises, and program expenses—within the whole parish budget.

Three months into the sabbatical, the parish's interim administrator called Fr. Martin to tell him that faculty members had stirred up parents to increase faculty salaries, and parents were meeting in one another's homes to garner support. The principal, he told the pastor, was meeting with the parent groups and agreed with their point of view.

By phone, Fr. Martin laid out with the interim administrator and with the trustees principles for settling parent concerns that allowed for an unanticipated but just salary increase.

Fr. Martin refrained from contacting the pastoral associate for education/principal, however, because his breach of Fr. Martin's trust may have led to an angry exchange that could have thwarted the process. The pastoral associate for education/principal made no explanatory call to Fr. Martin either.

When the interim administrator and councils settled their work, Fr. Martin initiated a frank discussion with the pastoral associate. Fr. Martin made it clear that, though the raised salaries would redound to some benefit, the pastoral associate had violated his responsibility to publicly support a budget he had consensually agreed to with the councils and had broken trust with the pastor and councils also by publicly siding with the parents.

Comprehending the relationship rupture and its meaning for his future effectiveness, the pastoral associate for education/principal took the initiative to resign.

The School Ministry Commission

For policy and practice, ministry, and money, the pastoral associate for education/principal establishes a school ministry commission to help focus, guide, and monitor the school ministry. It parallels the parish's councils and commissions in its function, membership term and selection, and exercise of leadership on behalf of the school ministry.

The school ministry commission belongs to the pastoral associate for education/principal. It assists with the basics of school ministry planning, which include:

* forging a school ministry mission statement complementary to the whole parish,
* shaping school ministry goals and objectives complementary to the whole parish,
* developing budget scenarios that help the finance council set tuition and recommend salary raises,
* offering staff expansion or contraction options that support curriculum development,
* establishing code of conduct policies so they reflect the school's unique personality and Gospel ministry standards, and
* setting school ministry goals regarding enrollment.

A Final Word

Consensus about the purpose of a parish school has broken down in our time, and a new consensus has yet to be achieved.

Meanwhile, a parish's school ministry remains a marvelous opportunity. If the religion curriculum is deeply rooted in the heart of the Tradition—the Scriptures, Jesus, Creed, sacraments, liturgy, and the vast sweep of Church history—then students can inspire their parents to engage in their faith formation and perhaps Sunday Eucharist as the students merely ask their parents for help with religion homework.

Indeed, one of the critical functions of a parochial school is long-term. Memories of school ministry worship, religious education, spiritual formation, pastoral care, community life, and Catholic culture—even after years of being away from church—can surface later to invite people back to the life of faith and the table of the Lord.

In Sum

The enormous richness of possibilities for a parish's school ministry warrants clear articulation of the school's mission as a ministry of the parish, mutually respectful structuring of the relationship between the pastoral associate for education/principal and the pastor and pastoral associates, and vigilant attention to the school's full integration into the parish's leadership and life. The mission of the Gospel calls us to this noble work not only for the short run but in hope of accomplishing God's transforming work for the ages.

JUST EMPLOYMENT PRACTICES

JUST EMPLOYMENT PRACTICES

Synodality and Just Employment

The Basic Dilemma

As a particular instance of the pilgrim people living in communion, spreading the Good News, and journeying to the Father, the parish is a people and place where heaven and earth meet in divine embrace. At the same time, the parish is a legal U.S. corporate entity with all the attendant privileges and responsibilities.

A Rough Example

Fr. Hannibal was appointed pastor of a 1,200-family parish-with-a-school in serious difficulty. The school parents, up in arms over an unexpected 37% tuition hike for the next year, were threatening to take their children out of the school. The school ministry was overstaffed—three full-time teachers taught a kindergarten enrollment of 18 students—and the principal, terminally ill with cancer, had been increasingly absent from the school over three years. The endowment had been depleted by 60% in the past five years to pay down the $2 million debt. The newly hired business administrator could find no record of how much money the parish owed to vendors or sat in the bank.

Fr. Hannibal huddled with the trustees and councils and began systematic, stabilizing work. By the end of three years, school ministry enrollment had settled at one-half the previous levels, the endowment had been secured, and the parish knew what it owed and held and was paying its bills. A parish staff of 42 had been reduced to 28, and 16 of these were new hires. In this massive staff change, only one case of employment arbitration arose, and that ended in a split decision that parish insurance covered.

All the while, of course, Fr. Hannibal presided at the Eucharist, preached, baptized, witnessed marriages, buried the dead, and visited the sick, parish families, and the school children.

The Parish and Corporate Reality

From the corporate point of view, every parish is a small business. The average U.S. parish with a school, for instance, would own $12 million in property, have a cash flow of over $2.5 million, employ 40 people, maintain 60,000 square feet of space on an acre of property, and have approximately 2,400 immediate stakeholders.

This corporate reality means that the community of faith is subject to many national and state laws and regulations. It also means that the pastor as CEO serves as the official employer for those who work for the parish corporation, with all the privileges and responsibilities that entails.

These corporate realities are fearsome and demanding. Because of the enormous impact it has on people's lives, the deep investment parishioners and staff have in one another, and the profound justice implications of it, no element of the parish's corporate responsibilities is more freighted than employment. The ramifications of the parish's being an employer touch all the parish's ministries.

The Question of Justice Frames and Pierces the Dilemma

Consequently, every parish's pastoral leadership group and assembly must confront what its employment responsibilities demand of the parish as a co-responsible community on Gospel mission.

The focus question for the employment dilemma might best be this: what is justice in employment for a Catholic parish? More helpfully, what is the right order of relationship between employer and employees for building the common good for our whole parish community?

A Contextual Note

Because of its responsibility for and legal relationship with each parish within it, every diocese establishes policy that governs employer/employee relationships. So does every parish. This policy is ordinarily articulated in a handbook available to all employees. These are corporate documents with an ecclesial subtext.

"At-Will" or "Just Cause" Employment?

Diocesan employment policies declare that the diocese/parish is either an "at-will" or a "just cause" employer.

* An "at-will" employer may end an employment relationship at any time for most any dissatisfaction.

* A "just cause" employer may end an employment relationship only in the following cases:

    * a reduction in force (RIF) – action taken when the financial health of the organization is strained to the point of jeopardy.

    * progressive discipline leading to dismissal—an extended process of listening, discussion, standard setting, and performance measurement which can lead to employee dismissal.

    * Just cause termination—when an employee transgresses specified legal and moral limits, e.g., stealing.

What follows takes the stand that whatever the diocesan legal employment policy, and whatever lawyers advise, Gospel justice demands that all church entities behave in practice not as an "at-will" but as a "just cause" employer.

Employment Contract or Employment Letter?

Employment is a relationship. An employee agrees to offer services. In exchange, an employer offers financial and benefits compensation, assistance for performing the assigned job well, and reasonable job security.

* The written and signed employment contract frames this relationship for a specified period.

* The written and signed employment letter frames this relationship as indefinite.

What follows takes the stand that an employment letter is preferable to a contract in a parish.

The contractual setting of a relationship terminus from the beginning, with some exceptions, sets limits that imbue the relationship with the stress of uncertainty and can lead to the abuses of manipulation by the employer or employee and at-will dismissal. The one-year contract, typical of educational settings, is a particularly notorious instrument for such abuses.

The employment letter leans toward covenantal relationship. Carefully hiring the proper person for the job, setting clear performance standards, offering careful and regular supervision, and strongly encouraging collaboration in the exercise of ministry—these attitudes and behaviors establish mutual listening, co-responsibility, and accountability; offer job security for the employer and employee; and set the stage for partnership and mutual trust in mission.

We Should Be Different

Right-ordering of relationships to build up the common good stands as a central Gospel call to conversion. It is also a central commitment of the Tradition. Consequently, justice in employment needs to stand as both a witness and commitment to Gospel integrity for a community of faith.

JUST EMPLOYMENT PRACTICES

Covenant Ministry

Three Justice Practices That Preserve Covenant Employment

Two texts and one form of regular dialogue characterize just employment practice and envelop it with the assurances of covenant relationship. The texts are the ministry description and the employment policies handbook. The ongoing dialogical element of covenant employment is ministry planning and review.

These three components of the employment relationship bless freedom, offer security, and integrally assist in fulfilling the needs of both employer and employee in the parish.

The Ministry Description

The efficient and effective functioning of any organization depends on clear and detailed job descriptions for its people. In the parish context, the ministry description:

* clarifies precise job requirements for the position during the composition process before the hiring,

* offers the applying minister a clear sense of the position's requirements,

* serves as a standard for performance measurement,

* and provides the employee and supervisor an ongoing basis for analyzing the expansion, contraction, and effectiveness of

    * the position,
    * the employee,
    * and the interrelatedness of all ministry positions.

A clear, detailed ministry description articulates the general purpose of a position, its specific tasks, and its co-responsibility and accountability relationships. Well-wrought, it serves as a measuring stick for ministry analysis.

In a mutual dialogue between supervisor and employee, ministry descriptions may also evolve. Parishes need change. Employee interests and capacities expand. New ministry opportunities arise. Used well for ongoing discussion, ministry description clarity in mutual dialogue can nip performance and requirement concerns in the bud, alert the employee and supervisor to ministry structure matters that need addressing, smooth ministry development in the parish, and build a trusting relationship between a supervisor and employee and among a whole staff.

Careful ministry descriptions and regular dialogue about position and personal evolution save time and energy that can be wasted in what can become personally painful and legally messy controversies.

Carefully wrought ministry descriptions are indispensable in the parish.

Meeting the Challenge is Worth It

Diedre was hired as a full-time parish secretary for the All Holy Angels Catholic Community, a merger of five small country parishes. The AHACC's only full-time employee, she received minimal direction from five pastors over 11 years.

As Fr. Joe became Diedre's sixth pastor, it quickly became apparent that he was disinclined to supervise Diedre. Rather than offer her clear limits and direction, he moved his office to the rectory. As he did so, Diedre began calling herself "office manager" and quit accepting guidance from her formal supervisor, the business administrator, who was part-time. Having succeeded in making that shift without reprimand, Diedre then called herself "assistant to the pastor." Fr. Joe shrugged both moves off, as well as their implications. At the same time, he allowed Diedre to become the only doorway to the pastor: her phone line and answering machine were the parish's only access to him. With all calls coming to her, Diedre began taking the initiative to deal with concerns that might otherwise have come to the pastor's attention. In the process, she established broader relationships within, and gained fuller information about the parish, further enhancing the power of her position.

Fr. Joe knows he needs to sit down with Diedre and review her written and unwritten title acquisitions and mushrooming informal ministry description. Confident of his power, however, and hating conflict, he demurs. Meanwhile, Diedre, defending all her moves as an effort to serve and lead because of the pastor's lack of availability, continues to insert herself, according to her preferences, in every area of the parish's ministry.

A Parish Employment Bible

The parish's Employment Policies Handbook is the employment bible for a pastor, a supervisor of other ministers, the HR office of the diocese, and the attorneys who work with pastors and parishes.

Pastors and supervisors of staff members, in consultation with the pastor, only exercise employment authority within the confines of published diocesan and parish employment policies. Typically, the pastor either adheres to handbook policies or loses the parish's right to insurance and risks suit. This cold reality gives employment supervisors a huge incentive to follow the parish's stated procedures, which incorporate the diocese's employment policy requirements as well.

Moreover, the Employment Policies Handbook serves as the employment bible for every parish staff member. It is given to every parish employee upon hiring and whenever it is revised.

Parish staff members can suffer terrible losses because of their ignorance of fundamental points made in the handbook. Repeated refusal to honor a supervisor's specific requests, for instance, or taking candy from school snack supplies when you have been asked not to do so—no one can stubbornly do these things and keep their job. One employee in a reduction in force, for example, assumed the parish broke a contract. She refused to sign a severance agreement and took legal action. An arbitrator ruled against the employee because the handbook provided for a reduction in force. The employee lost thousands of dollars because the handbook sat unread in a pile somewhere.

Leadership Engagement with the Handbook

The importance of the Employment Policies Handbook dictates that its composition and contents ought not to be considered an administrative matter left to the pastor or the diocese and the pastor alone.

Since it articulates the limits of what the pastor and ministry supervisor can and cannot do in the employment relationship, draws boundaries for supervisory relationships for all staff members, and offers guidelines for an employee's exercise of authority on many levels, both the finance and pastoral councils need to be involved in the parish handbook's approval process.

Parishioner leadership participation in handbook composition and monitoring offers the parish significant expertise in the composition process, greater assurance that the parish's policies are just and balanced for employees, and confidence for the parish staff and assembly if controversy arises.

Gospel Ministry Opportunity

The effort to make parish employment a written covenant reality offers pastoral leaders and the parish wonderful opportunities. It calls everyone to reflect on Gospel values and Church Tradition, dialogue about them, and discern common agreement about leadership priorities in employment. The process invites everyone to grow in the personal virtue of justice, asking themselves and one another: what is the right order of relationship that builds the common good toward the Kingdom?

Grappling with American cultural conflict with the Gospel, therefore, is integral to parish pastoral leadership. It serves as a gift that calls everyone to a deeper understanding of their cultural and ecclesial roots and a more reflective personal reconciliation of these roots deep within. ∎

JUST EMPLOYMENT PRACTICES

Ministry Planning & Review

The Third Justice Practice of the Employment Relationship Covenant

Pastors and pastoral associates supervise other parish staff members so they will perform effectively in the workplace. What constitutes quality supervision, therefore, needs to be a carefully considered high priority for those who exercise a supervisory role.

Performance Appraisal Versus Performance Analysis

Performance appraisal, a common form of supervision in business and many parishes, is an "over/under" relationship in which one person assumes power over another and makes judgments. Research indicates that appraisal typically effects no change in employee performance; it can even make things worse.

Performance analysis, on the other hand, is a form of employee supervision that helps a person become more effective in producing results.

As a method, performance analysis assumes that the parish as an organic system either contributes to or hinders effective ministry performance. The purpose of performance analysis is to help shape the employee's ministry, the supervisor's, and the entire parish system into a single, collaborative organism of effective communion in mission.

Carried out in an ongoing, collaborative planning process, this diagnostic approach to job performance in ministry:

* clarifies job expectations,
* offers perspective on contextual and performance weaknesses,
* elicits the reasons for weaknesses,
* mutually adjusts expectations,
* and deepens the trust relationship between the supervisor and the staff member.

The Purpose of Performance Analysis

Performance analysis aims to develop competencies in a staff member and do so in context, hoping that the analysis—supervisor and employee together—will strengthen team relationships and performance planning.

Performance analysis assumes that everyone on a parish staff, co-responsibly working in collaboration, contributes to effective or ineffective ministry functioning. The analysis seeks to build the staff and community for ministry and mission by aligning staff performance objectives with results.

The Steps of Performance Analysis

This process has specific steps. First, the parish staff member plans his or her work activities:

* developing an outline of job responsibilities with a time allotment for each;
* gathering job responsibilities under "key result areas," which serve as the organizing principles for the ministry;
* and then negotiating a plan with the supervisor to garner support.

The plan is then carried out, and a simple time-use record is kept.

At the end of each quarter, work responsibilities and the time invested to accomplish them are reviewed by the employee and the supervisor together.

In reciprocal listening and dialogue, achievements and areas that need improvement are listed. Blocking forces are noted. Improvement possibilities are proposed. Possibilities are negotiated to a conclusion for the next three months.

In sum, the collegial quarterly performance analysis session:

* reviews staff job responsibilities and the intended results,

* considers the proportion of the time expenditure,

* examines staff member achievements,

* reflects on blockages to ministry effectiveness,

* discusses possibilities for improvement,

* negotiates a plan for the next quarter,

* and strives for ministry collaboration and reliable supervisor support.

The Benefits of the Approach

However formally or informally done, this approach to supervision keeps everyone well-informed about what's happening in a given ministry area and with the minister, clarifies job responsibilities, maintains mutual accountability, opens mutual coaching possibilities, and keeps everyone regularly considering the shape of the parish's ministry, the ministry's evolution, and the minister's "fit" in context.

This approach also helps develop a teamwork approach to ministry built on shared insights and skills.

Covenant Employment: Collaborative Discernment and Evolving Transformation

However structured or unstructured performance analysis might be in a parish, if carefully done it will engage everyone in listening and dialogue about ministry, honor the dignity of everyone involved, and build communion in mission.

In a better way than performance appraisal, performance analysis incarnates and exemplifies, for the parish staff and the parish community, wide listening, honest dialogue, careful discernment, and the exercise of co-responsibility and co-accountability in mission. ■

JUST EMPLOYMENT PRACTICES

Covenant Hiring

The Parish Hiring Process

Pastoral leadership, particularly the pastor, must be especially alert when hiring new parish staff members. A careful hiring process requires very worthwhile time and energy. Sloppiness drains the parish's emotional and financial coffers.

The hiring process is the point where search committee members who represent parish constituencies are especially valuable.

Parish Hiring Rules

* Applications are taken from people outside the parish.
* No immediate family of parish staff members need apply.
* A representative search committee interviews the candidates for hiring.
* The pastor is never a member of a search committee.
* No person whom the new hire will supervise is a committee member.
* The search committee recommends candidates to the pastor in priority ranking.
* The pastor hires from the ranking and in accord with it.
* If the process fails, the search committee's work continues.
* The search committee dissolves once the pastor hires or the process, by consensus, is deferred.

Pastoral Associate Hiring

The search committee for a pastoral associate ordinarily needs to include a trustee (in an independent corporation parish), a pastoral council member, a pastoral associate, and parishioners who are closely familiar with and impacted by the ministry area. Occasionally, a "member of the opposition" is wisely included on a pastoral associate search committee. A pastoral associate hiring committee might consist of seven people.

Administrative Staff Hiring

The search committee for hiring an administrative staff member ordinarily needs to include a pastoral associate and parishioners knowledgeable about the area of expertise for which the person is being hired, preferably members of a council or commission.

The search committee for a maintenance supervisor, for instance, requires a member of the finance council, the immediate supervisor(s), and parishioners deeply knowledgeable about maintenance. The search committee for a bookkeeper requires a similar configuration, including the trustee who is corporate treasurer (in an independent corporation parish). The committee for an administrative staff member is ordinarily no larger than five people.

Guidelines for the Process

A. Application

* Post the position opening through the diocesan network and local newspapers.
* Set the application deadline for three weeks.
* Let a written application form be brief.

B. Meanwhile, the search committee:

* composes the ministry description or reviews it for omissions or mistakes, then revises it,
* discusses and agrees upon the kind of person the parish needs in the position, and
* forges interview questions.

C. After the deadline, the search committee:

* reviews résumés to determine the candidates it wants to interview (usually no more than three),

* refines questions and develops scenarios for applicant response, and

* establishes a schedule for interviewing with the committee and others concerned, for touring facilities, and for meeting relevant people.

D. The search committee conducts interviews—asking each candidate identical, prepared questions—and follows up on answers as necessary for clarification.

E. The search committee meets to listen, dialogue, and achieve consensus about whom to hire, ultimately recommending candidates in priority order to the pastor.

F. The pastor:

* hires the new staff member in accordance with committee ranking recommendations,

* informs the committee,

* and introduces the new hire to the parish once the employment letter and other documents are signed.

G. The search committee dissolves.

The Pastor and Hiring

The pastor may sit in on the ministry description discussion for purposes of clarification, sit silently during the interviews for the final round of candidates, sit in on the final discussion that determines recommendation ranking, or all three. The pastor's presence can be helpful for the committee's dialogue and the pastor's understanding.

The pastor may also wish to interview the final candidates for a pastoral associate position so he, the candidates, and the search committee develop a sense of "fit."

Still, because the committee's purpose is to discern a person's objective congruence for the position and the parish and to make priority ranked recommendations of candidates to the pastor, the pastor is never a member of a search committee.

When the Process is Shortcut

In June, with the parish hall being renovated for its re-dedication and the classroom building still a mess, the Sts. Felicity and Perpetua maintenance supervisor resigned. Desperate to finish work and with little time for a hiring process, the pastor and principal asked a parishioner if he wanted the job. An independent jobber with fine building skills, he took the position then asked if the parish would hire his son to help get the work done.

After the first 90 days of probation, the new maintenance supervisor showed himself to be a lone wolf. He resented direction, had poor supervisory skills relative to his staff, favored his son over other employees, chafed when his favoritism was pointed out, and began leaking his disaffection to staff members and parishioners.

Subject to the formal employment disciplinary process surrounding all these matters, eight months into the job, the maintenance supervisor was helped to see that he needed to either resign or be terminated. He chose to resign.

The fallout in the parish, however—whisperings in corners, silent glares from the former supervisor and his family in and out of church, the withdrawing of some parishioners from friendly relationships with the pastor and principal—was painful for everyone.

NOTE!

Observing the above hiring rules and following this search committee process saves pastoral leadership and the parish significant headaches. Shortcutting the covenant hiring process always backfires.

JUST EMPLOYMENT PRACTICES

Just Compensation

Times Have Changed

Financial compensation for lay ecclesial ministers is a major commitment of parish life. With a school or without, a parish typically invests over 80 percent of its expenses in personnel. That is appropriate.

Be Aware of the Context

Because the standard of living differs from one area of the country to another, most dioceses have established standards for compensation. While there are occasional exceptions, and policies do demand scrutiny—one U.S. diocese, for instance, honors only five years of experience when an elementary teacher transfers from one school to another, no matter how many years of experience he or she has accrued, which is a patently unjust policy—you should generally follow the diocesan compensation standards.

For all the nobility of ministry in the Church, no church employee should ever be harmed by stingy compensation. Justice requires that all who work for the Church be compensated in proper proportion to their need, their employment responsibilities, and commonly accepted professional standards.

Be Generous with Benefits

The high cost of health insurance makes benefits especially costly for the parish.

Still, justice requires that generous health and dental insurance coverage be part of every full-time employment compensation package.

Some dioceses require health insurance for employees who work more than a particular number of hours per week, for instance, 25 hours. Individual states may also legally require it for a certain number of work hours per week. What-

ever may be necessary, generous parish coverage means that the person employed feels secure in the event of an accident, a passing condition, or a lingering illness, ideally with a small co-pay.

Family coverage should also be available and cheap for those who need it. Even the grade school principal or business administrator—positions with a large salary in a parish—cannot afford health insurance on a Catholic parish salary if he or she has five school-age children. In justice, the parish needs to be generous in offering family coverage.

Structuring jobs to be part-time so the parish need not pay benefits is baldly unjust.

Be Eminently Fair and Faithful

If the parish cannot compensate fairly, then it should not hire. Other arrangements can be made to fulfill the parish's needs. The employment relationship covenant justly demands that an employee's needs receive high priority.

JUST EMPLOYMENT PRACTICES
Just Termination

The Limits of Job Security

A parish strives mightily to offer staff members the freedom to use their talents, shape their ministry, and do their jobs well; the security of deliberate planning, honest and respectful feedback, and the setting of clear limits; and the meeting of staff members' needs by supplying the orientation, training, supervision, and resources to accomplish the tasks set out for them.

However faithful a parish may be to these commitments, there are exceptions to assured, indefinite employment:

✱ a reduction in force (an extreme measure taken for financial reasons),

✱ failed progressive discipline in the workplace,

✱ and just cause discharge.

While the supervisor and employee, in accord with the commonly recognized rights and responsibilities of each, may have worked out clear parameters and expectations of the job and may thoroughly know diocesan and parish employment policy, nonetheless, the parish sometimes faces employment relationship breakdown.

Handling employment relationship breakdown also demands just words and deeds from co-responsible and accountable members of a parish community.

Reduction in Force

A reduction in force (RIF) is an extreme measure. It requires the organization to give the employees formal written notification of their financial problems and a list of criteria for employee retention. The organization must then apply the standards based on objective data, inform the employee personally about the termination of the employment relationship, provide the employee an explanation of the criteria's application to the employee's situation, and include in the termination letter a listing of employees by age. Some form of severance usually accompanies release from employment.

The RIF is rare and applied only in exceptional circumstances. The process outlined above must be used in all its particulars, or the parish becomes vulnerable to legal action.

The RIF is a painful experience for everyone in the workplace and spills over into the parish community. The RIF is an extremely stabilizing action for a financially distressed parish.

The simple permissibility of a RIF suggests that all parish employees need to remain alert to the parish's overall financial stability and state and support its flourishing.

Failed Progressive Discipline

Supervisors impose progressive discipline when they feel discontent with an employee's performance and insufficient rectifying change occurs. It includes, at a minimum, an oral warning substantiated by documentation, a written warning outlining necessary changes, a disciplinary action (like suspension without pay), a final written warning that articulates precise criteria for performance improvement, and a time frame for that improvement.

Progressive discipline can eventually lead to dismissal, which typically requires the permission of an attorney, the diocesan HR office, and the mutual concurrence of both in the decision.

Progressive discipline, painful as it can be, need not move to termination, however. It can be a highly constructive wake-up call for an employee or a supervisor. The whole listening and dialogue process can clarify expectations, surface new information, change the operation for the better, and preserve a good employee.

For Instance

The bookkeeper at St. Matthew's went through the progressive discipline process to the final written warning. Fr. Pete, the pastor, asked to meet with her.

Understanding the grave threat to her employment that the meeting represented, the bookkeeper explained to Fr. Pete that the system was broken. She then detailed why what Fr. Pete asked of her was impossible.

The bookkeeper not only kept her job but the whole bookkeeping system was revised and improved when the parish finance council acted on the information the bookkeeper provided.

Discharge for Just Cause

Discharge for just cause without progressive discipline can occur in cases of illegal bias or harassment, theft, records falsification, endangering misconduct, insubordination, breach of professional ethics, use of controlled substances in the workplace, public conduct contradicting Church teaching and morals, or gross violations of the employer/employee relationship.

Discharge for just cause also typically requires the concurrence of the pastor, an attorney, and the diocesan HR office.

If an employee is released, he or she usually can appeal the decision to mediation and, ultimately, binding arbitration.

Every diocese also has a resolution of work-related issues policy that begins with an appeal to the immediate supervisor and can run up the Chancery chain of command to a diocesan conciliation process.

Parish pastoral leaders and the members of the parish's staff need to understand what constitutes misconduct in the workplace. The Employment Policies Handbook needs to delineate all such misconduct and the consequences for it clearly.

Again, for Instance

Fr. Severin has a dog. One evening, he came to his box among the staff in-house mailboxes to find there a baggie with dog feces in it. A pastoral associate had found the feces near and inside the church entry, collected it, and placed it, with a note, in the pastor's mailbox. He assumed the feces was from Fr. Severin's dog and chose this way of letting him know about it.

Fr. Severin was amazed that a colleague would do such a thing, especially one already in the process of progressive discipline. Still, he was unsure how to respond.

When he mentioned the incident to an attorney six weeks later while in the throes of the pastoral associate's last days of employment, she instantly quipped, "Why didn't you fire the person on the spot?"

"I didn't know I could!"

Fr. Severin ought to have known. The pastoral associate, too, ought to have known that his action was a gross violation of the employer-employee relationship.

Confidentiality

The protection of an employee's reputation demands confidentiality within a termination process.

While parish staff members and the parish assembly may widely know about the RIF, the specifics of a particular staff member's situation must remain confidential. An employee's discharge for the failure of progressive discipline or just cause release also demands confidentiality.

The political nature of discharge in a parish community, however, may require some limited communication with pastoral staff members or the councils. In such instances, invoking the category "just cause discharge" and referencing the Employment Policies Handbook for information about the process serves the employee's and the parish community's interests far better than sharing the case's specifics. ∎

BUILDING A PARISH ASSEMBLY

BUILDING A PARISH ASSEMBLY

Engaging the Parish Assembly

Reciprocal Listening and Dialogue in the Whole Parish

Synodality practices can build trust, support, and credibility for pastoral leadership and deepen the parish's Gospel mission. Integral to these practices: pastoral leadership invites the whole parish assembly's participation in focusing, guiding, and monitoring the parish's Gospel ministry.

That is, synodality practices require that a parish establish structures, occasions, modes, and processes for listening to all the parishioners, consulting with all of them about the parish's ministry, and engaging all of them in Gospel mission.

The parish, therefore, needs to maintain venerable relationship builders that engage the parish assembly. Pastoral leadership also owes the parish community financial and pastoral annual reports and complementary parish assemblies.

The Parish Bulletin

The bulletin stands as a convenient, brisk, throwaway read aimed to offer parishioners brief but stout content:

* information about parish events.
* teaching reflections on the liturgical seasons and concerns underneath national and universal Church issues, and
* exposure to the contours and accomplishments of the parish's ministries.

The bulletin offers parish pastoral leadership a rich opportunity every week to snag ongoing parishioner interest.

The Parish's Internet Sites

Through internet communications, the parish offers itself to the world artfully, thoroughly, provocatively, and playfully.

The design, colors, and images of a website portray the feel of the place and the people. The information shared here is easily accessible, simple, accurate, thorough, and inviting.

The images and information offered across all internet platforms must be utterly reliable and current. Posts demand continual updates regarding parish events, feature reflections, and meaningful personal and faith sharing if the communications are to engage browsing interest continually.

The sites also need to invite parishioner engagement and offer and receive prompt response in turn.

The bulletin and the web platforms require consistent review and engagement from pastoral leadership and staff. These modes for communicating also demand capable writers and editors who know their craft and the parish and who have sufficient competency and perspective to both communicate well and experiment with new possibilities.

Household Visits/Census

The pastoral leadership of territorial parishes needs to know the geography and demographics of the parish. Where people live shapes their relationship with the world and proclaims their priorities and concerns.

Knowing the neighborhood offers pastoral leadership perspective on the parishioners' economic strength and relationship patterns. A neighborhood's housing types; depth; proximity to open land, roadways, airports, and railroads; and proximity to services all help leadership understand parishioner identity.

The sociological and physical structure of the territory also offers perspective on the parishioners' relationship to the parish. For instance, a major thoroughfare may slice a neighborhood off from easy access to a parish or even awareness of it. Shallow and mixed neighborhoods, long drives for services, the church being downtown, and the parishioners living in the suburbs—location shapes a parish profoundly. Walking and driving the parish territory offers valuable angles on people's likely relationship with the parish.

Furthermore, engaging people in their homes is a pastoral priority. Accepting invitations to meetings in homes, enjoying a meal with a family or neighborhood, stopping by for parish census information, and visiting the sick and homebound are all venerable pastoral practices that offer beautiful opportunities for listening to people's hearts, opening dialogue with them, and laying the groundwork for focusing the parish's mission and widening its synodality practice.

Coffee and Donuts

Sunday hospitality after Mass is also a priority for pastoral leadership. Every Sunday.

"Coffee and donuts" holds risks. Many of the same folks show up week after week. The inclination to sit with one group or another instead of to greet everyone remains a constant temptation. The occasional unpleasant exchange, direct or observed, can be upsetting.

Nonetheless, the opportunities to come to know people, immediately engage their concerns, do some teaching, and welcome new people into the community far outweigh the risks.

Parish Organizations

Pastoral leadership must engage with parish organizations of all sorts: Men's Club, Women's Club, Teen Group, Knights of Columbus, Daughters of Isabella, Boys and Girls Scouts, etc.

Wise pastoral leadership assists these groups to keep clear about their purpose and supports them in fulfilling their mission within the parish's Gospel mission.

Consistently expressing gratitude for their service remains vital to sustaining healthy relationships and to the possibility of helping these groups focus their activity on the mission's behalf.

If they are parish groups, wise pastoral leadership monitors their financial practices. Best policy: the parish holds their money like a bank would, and the pastor signs their checks. ∎

BUILDING A PARISH ASSEMBLY

Two Annual Reports

Reports to the parish about its pastoral and financial activity and the opportunity to reciprocally listen and dialogue about that activity build trust and participation in Gospel mission for a parish community.

The Annual Financial Report

The financial report is published at the end of the parish's fiscal year, which for many ends on June 31. The report is often published in early fall.

Dioceses typically require parish financial reporting that accords with a chart of accounts the chancery promulgates for all parishes.

Often, a parish's financial report to parishioners will follow the diocesan chart of accounts. That usually proves unhelpful. Why? The diocese's chart of accounts serves its corporate report purposes, which require the diocese to shape a chart that will successfully organize account information for many parishes in various situations.

The Parish Financial Report Form

A financial report to parishioners needs to be immediately accessible and simply understandable.

Consequently, though usually extra work for the parish office and finance council, it is wise for parish leadership and better for the parish in general that leadership publish the annual financial report according to a commonsense chart of accounts.

Parishioners want to understand the parish's streams of income clearly: Sunday stewardship, bequests, other gifts, fees, sacramental services, tuition, endowment income and distributions, bequests, property sales, etc.

A Parish's Gospel Ministries

✱ worship (liturgy and liturgical music),

✱ religious education,

✱ charitable works,

✱ spiritual formation,

✱ pastoral care,

✱ community building/hospitality,

✱ justice, and

✱ administration

Parishioners want to understand the costs incurred for resident clergy salaries, clergy benefits, required diocesan clergy support, clergy living, clergy residence maintenance, assisting clergy, and clergy travel expenses. They want to understand the outlay for each ministry area: salary expenses, benefits, office expenses, continuing education costs, and travel expenses. They also want to know what the plant costs to maintain and the parish's contract services and capital expenses.

Each parish's size and situation represent unique challenges for a helpful annual report. Nonetheless, the yearly report should clearly show the parish's streams of income and what the parish and its ministries cost.

Moreover, the information presented needs to match meticulously, even if differing in account categories, the numbers reported to the diocese.

The document may be a separate report mailed to all parishioners, or it may be published in bulletin form. In whatever form, multiple copies need to remain available for some weeks in the vestibule, the offices, and the parish hall. Perhaps maintaining the posting on the parish website for a month or two would be wise.

The Parish Ministries Report

The annual ministries report offers accountability for the parish's ministries and pastoral mission.

Dioceses typically request annual statistics from the parish about the numbers of people in the programs of religious education, sacramental preparation, the school, and the Order of Christian Initiation for Adults; statistics about the numbers attending church each week, baptized, confirmed, admitted to Eucharist, anointed, married, and buried; and statistics about clergy and staff numbers and categories, and parish organizations and membership numbers. All these statistics ought to be shared each year with the parish.

The report might also include brief commentary that assesses—reporting from pastoral staff and pastoral council discussions—the parish's effectiveness in each of its ministries and its mission. Hopes for the future are wisely included as well.

This report is typically published at the end of the fiscal year, though its publication at the end of a calendar year is defensible. Like the financial report, this document may be a separate mailer to all parishioners, or it may be published in bulletin form and on the parish website. In whatever form it's published, multiple copies must remain available for some weeks in the vestibule, the offices, and the parish hall.

A Parish Assembly

Each of these reports strongly suggests the worthwhileness of a parish assembly.

The purpose of a parish assembly would be reciprocal listening and dialogue among pastoral leadership and parishioners about the parish's ministry life. This exchange aims to express accountability, transparency, co-responsibility, and participation that builds communion and trust in the parish and opens possibilities for fresh insight and new ministry direction.

A parish assembly might be a single event or multiple events after Masses. Whatever pastoral leadership chooses, the nature of a parish assembly (or assemblies) requires convenient scheduling, broad accessibility, careful listening, free exchange, and a generous time frame to engage everyone's concerns. It also suggests the resourcing and discerning presence of the pastor, councils, and pastoral staff.

The financial report, ministry report, and regular parish assemblies are fundamental and promising synodality practices for every parish.

BUILDING A PARISH ASSEMBLY

A Sample Data Gathering

For the Parish on the Peripheries

Yet another form of parish assembly might be a data gathering session or a series of them. This form of assembly might be scheduled yearly or, if the parish's agenda is full, every few years to assess emerging pastoral needs.

This approach might also be used with parish staff and organization groupings or with groups of people on the peripheries whom the parish seeks to engage and whose pastoral needs the parish seeks to understand.

Principles

The purpose of this kind of assembly or session is fourfold:

* Listening and dialoguing in a way that develops communion relationship.
* Gathering "reality on the ground" data about pastoral needs.
* Increasing pastoral ministry participation through awareness about the who, how, when, and where of meeting real pastoral need.
* Planning effective pastoral action.

What is gleaned from this sort of assembly is brought back to pastoral leadership and placed within a parish discernment process.

The Four Questions

The questions asked in a session are cast here for a parish assembly. They are easily modified for any group.

* What do you see as the strengths of the parish's life?
* What do you see as the weaknesses of the parish's life?

* What are the challenges to the parish's life?
* What are the hopes and dreams of this parish?

The Components of the Process

A data gathering session, or series of them, would ideally include the following components:

OPENING

* Prayer. The event might even begin with or follow Eucharist.
* Table fellowship. This fellowship might be a meal or beverages and a snack. The purpose of it is to create an atmosphere of ease and openness for listening and dialogue.

THE LISTENING PARISH

GROUP SHARING

* The leader(s) of the session then invites the assembled to break into discussion-size sub-groups. Each subgroup would be nine persons or less to facilitate listening and dialogue.
* The leader(s) then asks the sub-groupings to answer the four questions, each discussed one at a time.
* A recording secretary is designated within each group.
* The sub-groupings are invited to come to agreement about their answers to the question.
* Leadership circulates through the venue to help facilitate the subgroups, offering group process suggestions and perspective.

GATHERING THE DATA

* The data gathered under each question in each subgrouping is then brought forward and recorded by process leadership for the whole assembly's review. This step occurs either after each question is processed in the sub-groupings or after all the subgroups have processed all four questions.
* The data gathered from everyone under each question is then prioritized in open dialogue with the entire assembly. That is, process leadership invites all the assembled to come to preliminary agreement about the priorities evident in the data gathered. This exercise is fruitful and necessarily loose.

CLOSING

* Leadership explains to the assembly what will be done with the data.
* Leadership thanks the assembled for their participation.
* The session ends with brief prayer.

FOLLOW-UP

* Afterward, the data is collated and offered to the participants, parish pastoral leadership, and the parish assembly for further pondering.
* The data is brought to parish leadership to be funneled into the parish's discernment processes.
* The parish community remains informed about the continuing process as parish pastoral leadership formulates and executes that process.

Some Notes

The four simple questions have proven to reap enormous and helpful data for pastoral leadership and a parish. Indeed, bishops have used this process in parish visitations across the diocese to greatly benefit the parishes and the diocese.

Whether on newsprint or computer equipment, the sessions require public display of all the data gathered and processed.

Each session requires a small team, ideally three. One leads. Two others fill in gaps the leader may miss, circulate through the sub-groupings to assist in their process, and help ensure that everyone is heard in the subgroup and large group processes.

The main process leader must be a clear instructor, skilled listener, accountable sorter, and accurate recorder.

Finally, Remember Trust

Building trust and keeping it is fundamental to the process and the parish community. Many a data-gathering process has broken trust because its results vanished like dandelion seeds in the wind.

After the sessions or events are completed, pastoral leadership needs to remain rigorously transparent about what's being done with the data and be carefully accountable to the participants, pastoral leaders, and the parish assembly for the continuing process.

MOVING TOWARD THE PERIPHERIES

MOVING TOWARD THE PERIPHERIES

Opening to the Peripheries

The Call

Implementing synodality practices in the parish requires a first-order, laser-like focus on all the decision-making, decision-taking, and decision-implementation and evaluation processes within the parish. The reason for that priority is communion in mission, growing together in integrity and consistency of Gospel witness. In our time, all Church entities are called to make this growing and changing together as a united community a constant because the process constitutes our being and becoming church.

As Pope Francis made clear the day before his election, however, being church demands of us much more.

> Evangelizing presupposes a desire in the church to come out of herself. The church is called to come out of herself and go to the peripheries, not only geographically, but also the existential peripheries: the mystery of sin, of pain, of injustice, of ignorance and indifference to religion, of intellectual currents and of all misery.
>
> Cardinal Jorge Bergoglio, March 12, 2013

So, what does going out to the peripheries look like for the parish?

Listening to the Parish

Being church requires listening first to the parish community. Pastoral leadership needs to establish structures, occasions, modes, and processes for encountering, listening to, dialoguing with, and accompanying parishioners to meet their real needs and longings.

This listening and dialogue means grappling with all people's pastoral needs—Catholic or not—manifest within the geographical boundaries of the parish and accompanying them toward fulfilling their needs. Understanding the demographics and the economic and social conditions within the parish's boundaries focuses important questions: Who are the marginalized within the territory? Where are they? How can they be accessed, listened to, accompanied, and invited into a Gospel way of life?

This process, and all that follow, requires a special sensitivity to those experiencing poverty within this realm, which includes the financially, culturally, intellectually, and emotionally ostracized.

Listening to the Civic Community

Being church also means establishing structures, occasions, modes, and processes for listening to

THE LISTENING PARISH

the immediate civic community beyond the parish's boundaries. What pastoral needs manifest in the local area? In the state? The nation? Who are the marginalized and those experiencing poverty? Where are they? How can they be encountered, listened to, accompanied, and invited into a Gospel way of life?

Listening in the Diocese and the Church Universal

Gospel faithfulness in being church requires the parish to establish structures, occasions, modes, and processes for listening to the diocesan and universal church.

What are the ministry priorities of the bishop and the Bishop of Rome, church leadership groups, and church outreach ministries? Where do we find fracture within the church and people whose pastoral needs are neglected? How do we encounter and serve far-flung peoples whose priorities differ from ours? How do we build communion with our ecumenical brothers and sisters and accompany them? What pastoral needs manifest in the churches? Who are the marginalized and those experiencing poverty? Where are they? How can they be accessed, listened to, accompanied, and invited deeper into a Gospel way of life?

Listening to the Wide and Deep Concerns of the Parishioners

Being church also calls the parish to establish structures, occasions, modes, and processes for listening to the parishioners' cries of the heart: their concerns about matters from addiction to family breakage, political cleavage to economic stagnation, racial hostility and gun violence to civic elections, psychological and social isolation to retreat from committed faith. What pastoral needs manifest within the parishioners' longings and preoccupying concerns as they live their daily lives? Who are the marginalized and those experiencing poverty? Where are they? How can they be encountered, listened to, accompanied, and invited into a Gospel way of life?

Listening to the World

To be church, a parish community also needs to establish structures, occasions, modes, and processes for listening to the pastoral needs of the world: from the war-torn to those trapped in backwaters, from the migration of peoples to planetary climate change, from the immediate anguish we see on the news to people's trembling over long-term threats.

What pastoral needs manifest in the world? Who are the marginalized and those experiencing poverty? Where are they? How can they, too, be encountered, listened to, accompanied by us, and invited into a Gospel way of life?

So How do we Proceed?

Called to the pattern of life Jesus has shown us, being church calls the parish community to open its ears and its heart in a culture of encounter far beyond the concerns of self-preservation and accompanying all people of faith and people in the larger world as they strive to meet their real need.

But how can a parish respond to all that it hears? ■

MOVING TOWARD THE PERIPHERIES

Responding to the Peripheries

After Listening...?

Listening as church with a merciful heart calls the experience of parish to the experience of a culture of encounter: dialogue, pastoral discernment, decision, and accompaniment action.

Pastoral Dialogue

A responsive dialogical process engages pastoral leadership, the parish assembly, and those on the peripheries whose needs have been heard, at least in a preliminary way, and whose necessities call for pastoral accompaniment.

The structure of this dialogical process would be largely experimental. That is, multi-faceted and effective means, modes, and processes need to be considered and tried to meet the gifts and aspirations of the local parish community.

The dialogue process best aims to be widely participative and inclusive.

Synodality practice within a culture of encounter invites all participants to engage differing viewpoints face-to-face in an environment of acceptance, expressing and listening to all viewpoints with openness to learning new ways of seeing and valuing. This necessarily reciprocal process aims to lead participants to find links to structures and channels for accompaniment responses aligned with the Gospel.

Pastoral Discernment

Walking the synodal path demands that the totality of the faithful—pastors and people together in horizontal relationship—make together, in a culture of encounter, the decisions that shape the mission. The discernment process entails, therefore, finding methods and structures that help the faith community eventually achieve consensus around the mission.

Discernment includes assessing limits:

* Who are the priority people and groups we as a parish seek to encounter and perhaps accompany?
* What are the realistic possibilities for the parish and those to and with whom the parish engages?
* What are the parish's priorities?
* What are the need priorities?
* How might pastoral leaders, parishioners, and those on the peripheries strive together to accompany one another and achieve common aims?
* What time frame is required?
* What is the likely cost?
* How does the parish obtain the necessary resources?
* What would be the shape of the parish's accompaniment?
* What would be the parish's commitment?
* How do the possibilities and given choices integrate the parish and those on the peripheries with Gospel mission in an ongoing culture of encounter?

Culture of Encounter

> I prefer a church which is bruised, hurting, and dirty because it has been out on the streets, rather than a church which is unhealthy from being confined and from clinging to its own security.
>
> Pope Francis, November 10, 2015

This kind of discernment process might be extended and demanding. It must be carefully shaped, requiring rules, creativity, experimentation, and flexibility on many levels. It would also demand patience and a keen sensitivity to the rising up of personal agendas and the temptation to stall action.

Such engagement constitutes a culture of encounter and builds the parish and the Church. The process of this messy encounter transforms everyone in the light of the Gospel.

What is Consensus?

Because of the embracing engagement of pastoral leadership, the parish assembly, and those on the peripheries, the discernment process needs to include decision-taking about what constitutes consensus:

✸ Is it unanimity?

✸ Is it 90% agreement of all the participants together?

✸ Is it 90% agreement of all the participants together and 90% agreement of certain constituent groups consenting separately, and 100% agreement of some groups?

The Discernment Questions

Participants need to be reminded that the process is fundamentally spiritual. The agreement that listening, dialogue, and discernment seek to bring about is always subject to two fundamental questions:

✸ What does God want of us?

✸ Can I live with the decision?

Decision-Taking

The gradually building process of consensus decision-taking evokes communion of mind and heart. Moreover, as participants in the consensus-building process discern the Holy Spirit's truth about their missionary path, consensus decisions become binding for all—pastors, pastoral leaders, the parish assembly, and those on the peripheries... all together.

Implement the Decision

Once the sorting is done and agreement is achieved, leadership, parishioners, and those on the peripheries exercise their co-responsibility and express their communion by accompanying one another and putting decision into action.

Implementing a decision requires that participants remain alert to internal and external affirmation of the decision within their common and complementary action. It also requires in the execution steps alert and continual reshaping of the accompaniment action so the common goals are achieved or are continually refocused.

Evaluate

The participants and the whole parish assembly then exercise their transparent, accountable co-responsibility by submitting the action to mechanisms, modes, and processes of evaluation to improve it, redirect it, reframe it, or reconsider it. The evaluation results and expectations for the future are then reported to the parish assembly for review.

The Completion of the Circle

Evaluation completes the synodality practices circle because it is a listening encounter. Thus, within the evaluation, the whole communion-building synodality process is refreshed as participants continue the never-ending journey of being church, accompanying one another and those in need on Gospel mission in a culture of encounter.

✸

MOVING TOWARD THE PERIPHERIES

A Large Group Listening Process

The Synod Model

The Synod on Synodality required a process that would be effective with and for over 365 participants. It offers us an effective model that might well be adapted for a parish setting.

The Process Itself

The process the Synod followed taxed some of its participants. Interestingly, the lay participants found the process more natural and agreeable than some of the ordained. Perhaps daily immersion in family is the best preparation for synodal practice. It is helpful to remember that when we implement synodal practices, we are simply striving to be family together.

A structural note: at the Synod, every conversation table of ten had a designated facilitator and a secretary. The role of the facilitator was to keep time and safeguard everyone's participation. The secretary was the recorder and presenter of the group discussion.

The Synod's process, re-framed for the parish, follows:

1. Prayer

The Synod began with an ecumenical prayer service, a three-day retreat reflecting on the dispositions of faith and practice required for participating well, and a Eucharist.

Beginning with prayer sets the stage for entrusting the whole process to God's tender care and enlarging the participants" hearts toward detached listening. This opening prayer best includes some form of reflection on what dispositions of faith need to be in place for synodal listening.

The retreat master, Fr. Timothy Radcliffe, O.P., reflected on topics such as: do not be afraid, but open in hope; be alert that our understandings of the Church as home differ; we move forward reaching for friendship with the Lord and each another; remember that conversation is an art; remember that anger arises from fear, so gently address the fear; dare to face the truth and trust in the Holy Spirit.

> If we let ourselves be guided by the Spirit of truth, we shall doubtless argue. It will sometimes be painful. There will be truths we would rather not face. But we shall be led a little deeper into the mystery of divine love and we shall know such joy that people will be envious of us for being here, and we shall long to attend the next session of the Synod!
>
> Timothy Radcliffe, O.P., October 3, 2023

Note that all prayer for synodality practice needs to be intentional, not heavy-handed, but graciously aimed to offer space for the Spirit's work and offer encouragement or stimulus for the participation of everyone. A thoughtful, astute planning group is required for structuring prayer interventions.

2. Lay Out the Question

Each consideration for the whole assembly is offered to the participants in a little talk that focuses the question for them.

This reflection on the question allows participants around the tables to begin their sharing and listening by considering their thoughts and feelings in relation to the question.

3. Share about the Question

Each person is then given four minutes to share his or her perspective from their thought and prayer. This sharing is generally more about communicating experiences than making arguments.

This listening step ends with a few minutes of silent prayer and reflection.

4. Share about What Struck You

Each participant then offers a brief, two-minute reflection on what resonated or sparked internal resistance in what they heard. No judgments are made. All simply listen.

This step is also followed by a brief period of silent prayer and reflection.

5. Open Dialogue

This open time of conversation seeks to recognize intuitions and agreements, to identify disagreements and points of discord, to note new questions, and to allow new insights to emerge.

The purpose of this time is not to force agreement but to comprehend the breadth and contours of the participants' responses to the question.

6. Report to the Assembly

In this step, the secretary from each group collates and reports the group's experience to the whole assembly.

Whether the group forges the report together or entrusts the report composition to the secretary, the secretary needs to be careful to reflect and represent in the report everyone in the small group.

7. Process the Reports in the Small Groups

After listening to all the reports, the small groups meet again to reflect together on what they have heard in the assembly.

They then distill together the fruits of the assembly session and formulate a group report that includes proposals for the next steps. This report is offered to the coordinating group

8. The Coordinating Group Frames the Next Steps

The coordinating group takes the reports, reflects on them, and determines potential next steps in the process. Those steps might be tabling discussion of some topics, movement toward a decision, continuing the process with a new question, or a modified direction for the whole process.

Whatever the sense of the coordinating group, their inclinations, intuitions, and proposals need to be formulated for the whole assembly as a proposal.

9. General Consensus around the Next Movement

The coordinating group then brings forward to the whole assembly their proposals for the next steps and asks for the assembly's consent. The result of the assembly consensus may be agreement on the next question, or consensus that there is no consensus.

Whatever the conclusion of the attempt to achieve assembly consensus, the process starts over with the next question, even if that question is about the steps required for moving forward to achieving consensus for moving forward.

Remember…

The aim of implementing synodality practices in the parish is not decisions. Rather, synodality practices nourish our coming together and being together as church.

That is, if we embrace the beauty of God and the beauty of our striving together to grow in harmony, if we honor the goodness of God and the goodness of all men and women as God has created them, and if we honestly accept God's truth and the truth of the lives of the pilgrim people with whom we share faith, then we are abiding within a genuine experience of God and an authentic experience of Church. We are being the family of God in all its marvelous diversity, walking on pilgrimage together in faith, hope, and love.

A SAMPLE PASTORAL PLANNING PROCESS

A SAMPLE PASTORAL PLANNING PROCESS

Process Outline

Introduction

What follows is a "do-it-yourself" kit for planning based on a system developed by Dr. Robert G. Smith of Ohio State University. It is designed to help one person, or several people, plan anything.

The process has been effective with college administrators and college students, with graduate school faculty, and with parishioners on councils. It has proven enormously helpful for doing comprehensive, whole parish planning or individual ministry planning.

The Keys to the Process' Effectiveness

There are two keys to this process' effectiveness.

First, the whole process—and every session within it—needs to be understood as spiritual discernment. It aims to discern what God wants of the parish community. The process should begin and end with prayer, punctuating any difficult moments. Continual reminders about the umbrella question help immensely: what does God want of us?

Second, the process needs to be well led by a critical-thinking coordinator who understands the process, listens with discernment, accurately reports and helps clarify participants' contributions, remains alert to group consensus, can ask forward-moving questions, and stays detached from the process' outcomes. Moreover, because the process can be tedious, especially in the early stages, the coordinator needs to know when to call it quits for a given session and when prayer can most effectively complement difficult moments.

The Basic Process

Long-range planning (three to five years) aims to establish as high a correlation as possible between who we are, what we are thinking, and what we are doing. This requires that we understand our values, mission, and priorities and then gather data to recognize past and present trends in our experience so we can provide an intelligent framework for future development.

Since the proof of the process' effectiveness lies in the process itself, the best way to understand what follows and test its worth is to take a single, simple area of present concern, work it through the planning process, and see what happens.

The basic steps of the process follow.

Clarify Our Community's Identity: What Do We Think We are Doing?

STEP 1: DESCRIBE THE PARISH'S SENSE OF ITSELF.

✱ Describe the parish's basic beliefs, its values, as a distinct community.

✱ Describe the parish's understanding of its basic purpose, its mission.

✱ Describe the parish's understanding of its basic functions.

Clarify Our Community's Image: What Conditions Parish Activity?

STEP 2: DESCRIBE PARISH RESOURCES AND CONSTRAINTS.

* Describe and chart the parish's organizational structures.
* Describe its basic policies.
* Describe the parish's main characteristics.
* Designate what characteristics are strengths.
* Designate what characteristics are weaknesses.
* Describe environmental factors that impact the parish.
* Describe assumptions about the parish's future.

Articulate Our Community's Direction: What Do We Intend to Do?

STEP 3: FORMULATE GOALS AND OBJECTIVES.

* Establish general three-year or five-year goals.
* Establish specific, measurable objectives underneath the goals.

Articulate Accomplishment: How Are We Going to Do It?

STEP 4: COLLECT DATA ON INTENDED OBJECTIVES AND ANALYZE TRENDS.

* Collect data for accomplishing the goals.
* Analyze trends that impact achieving the goals.
* Note planning gaps.

STEP 5: DESIGN PROGRAMS TO ACHIEVE THE STATED OBJECTIVES.

* Establish general strategies for accomplishing each goal.
* Design alternative programs as backup possibilities.
* Assign action responsibility for achieving the goals and the objectives.

STEP 6: ALLOCATE THE NECESSARY RESOURCES.

* Do a budgetary analysis and estimate the needed resources for the process.
* Allocate resources.

STEP 7: COORDINATE AND SCHEDULE ACTIVITIES TO ACHIEVE THE STATED OBJECTIVES

* List the necessary activities for accomplishing the goals and the objectives underneath them.
* Establish an implementation schedule for these activities.
* Coordinate the planning components.

STEP 8: REVIEW AND EVALUATE PROGRAMS IN TERMS OF THE INTENDED OBJECTIVES AND RECYCLE THE RESULTS.

* Review the resulting actions.
* Evaluate their effectiveness.
* Modify activities that have yielded unsatisfactory outcomes.
* Use the resulting learning from the process of planning and execution to begin a planning process anew.

A SAMPLE PASTORAL PLANNING PROCESS

Step 1: Parish Sense of Self

The Strength of this Process Model

This model of planning is a top-down process. Though it includes critical bottom-up exercises in later stages, the process begins with the planning group clearly stating what it thinks the parish is doing from a philosophical, theoretical point of view. If the parish makes the effort to understand its identity and image clearly, then it can better assess if its actions line up.

This planning method aims to be both deepening and transformational. It invites the parish's administration to be accountable for present reality, the planning group to review and evaluate the parish's current practices, and parish leadership to move the parish toward co-responsible and accountable best practices consistent with its self-understanding and the mission.

Clarifying our Community's Identity, What We Think We Are Doing

The process begins with the group writing out what it understands to be the fundamental identity of the parish: its values and priorities, its sense of its mission within the Christian mission, and its resulting ongoing activities.

This first step demands the planning group move underneath credal formulations and pieties. Rather, the planning group best focuses its attention on the particular community within the larger Gospel mission: its people; its sense of its ministry priorities because of its location, size, and history; and its sense now of the community's direction and what it might best accomplish.

Note: this step, done in a synodal style, demands listening and dialogue within the planning group—typically the pastoral council, including the pastor, but also between the planning

group and the pastoral staff, other parish leaders, and the parish assembly. Wide consultation and participation throughout the process is not only politically wise but spiritually transforming as consensus about the community's identity builds.

STEP 1: Describe the Parish's Sense of Itself.

DESCRIBE THE PARISH'S BASIC BELIEFS AND VALUES AS A DISTINCT COMMUNITY.

The planning group lists the widely accepted convictions that, without much debate, state the community's values and their relative weight. These values provide a foundation for planning. Getting them right is of central importance and tricky.

THE LISTENING PARISH

Whether the planning group is large (never more than 15) or small, this step will likely feel confusing, be time consuming, and will require considerable vocabulary and statement revision. A satisfying, congruent set of beliefs statements often takes six to eight sessions to accomplish, sometimes more. Synodal style suggests, at a minimum, publishing the listing and engaging parish leadership and assembly feedback in listening and dialogue.

The result should be about six to eight consensus values statements in priority listing.

DESCRIBE THE PARISH'S UNDERSTANDING OF ITS MISSION.

The planning group then forges a broad, comprehensive statement describing the parish's ongoing purpose.

After the beliefs work, the composition of a statement that captures the mission thrust of this parish community within the larger Gospel mission usually flows. Including engaging parish leadership and assembly feedback, three to four sessions may be required to finalize it.

The result should be a simple statement of about two to four lines. Done well, the statement can feel like poetry.

DESCRIBE THE PARISH'S UNDERSTANDING OF ITS BASIC FUNCTIONS.

The planning group then lists out the separate, major, ongoing activities of the parish in broad strokes.

Though the listing may be long, this step also flows easily. It might take three sessions to accomplish, including parish engagement.

The resulting listing is most often an eye-opener for the planning group and the parish at large.

While all parishes share some identity elements—all worship, all have catechetical programs, all reach out to the neighborhood, etc.—the inner-city parish differs in values, mission, and activities from the rural parish, the adult-oriented downtown parish differs from the family-oriented suburban parish, and the parish of 10,000 households differs from the parish of 50 households.

Every parish community aims to embrace the universal mission through the unique gifts of the particular people, place, and time of *this* community of the people of God.

Publish the Results

The resulting statements of this first step of the process are published to the whole parish community. The mission statement might be placed permanently in the bulletin and on the website. The other listings may be published permanently on the website and be shared periodically in the bulletin. ■

A SAMPLE PASTORAL PLANNING PROCESS

Sample Beliefs Statements

Background on the Samples

The beliefs statements below were composed by pastoral councils and affirmed by faith communities in inner-ring suburban neighborhood parishes with schools. In each setting, the beliefs statements, though seemingly innocuous, represent transformative listening and dialogue through the composition process.

St. Albert's Beliefs

At its founding in 1930, St. Albert's first and deeply symbolic act was to erect a school building and situate there both the parish's worship and education. The church building was erected 22 years into the parish's life. As a result, this community's commitment to its school became so strident that it believed its mission was the school. Consequently, the parish's worship life was shallow, its adult and community faith formation was thin, its ministry participation was spare, and its commitment to charity and justice ministry was superficial. The parent and teacher community saw and marketed the school as Christian rather than Catholic and private rather than parish. Sunday stewardship flowed at a trickle. The school's financial sustainability was at high risk.

St. Albert's beliefs statement composition and priority-setting process began an extended transformation of minds and hearts. The parish's affirmation of the statements was, in context, monumental, even if many parishioners only gradually came to understand.

BELIEFS STATEMENTS

* The parish community's gathering to celebrate Eucharist is where St. Albert shares most deeply our communion with God and one another.

* The parish community sees the ministry of Jesus as the source of our beliefs and the Scriptures and teaching of the Catholic Church as the guide for our lives.

* Through our participation in sacramental life and our relationship with the bishop, we share in the universal communion that is the Catholic Church.

* We believe that the Holy Spirit moves with and binds together all men and women of faith.

* Prayer is a gift from God and taught by Jesus Christ. As a praying community, St. Albert seeks to support people in every state of mind and walk of life.

* St. Albert strives to create a sense of belonging by being a welcoming community that extends hospitality, recognizes people's gifts, and works to build unity.

* We believe that all members of our community, whatever their age or way of life, have been gifted by God with a call to worship, fellowship, service, and Christian leadership and to the imitation of Christ in all we do.

* As a parish community we are coming to understand that God profoundly gifts us, and that stewardship is fundamentally a sharing of our varied gifts in praise and thanks to God, the Giver.

* We are committed to stimulating the growth of lay leadership across the parish and its ministries.

* St. Albert is committed to assisting the full range of parishioners in learning about, internalizing, and deepening their commitment to faith and to involving as many as possible in the shaping of parish education and formation programs.

* As witnessed by our school, the St. Albert community is committed to the education of

THE LISTENING PARISH

our children and their formation in Christian faith and values.

✸ St. Albert believes it essential that many parish ministries be family-oriented to provide support and to ground the experience of family in faith.

✸ St. Albert strives to support, be present to, and respond to parishioners in any spiritual or practical need.

Mary, Queen of Peace's Beliefs

Mary, Queen of Peace was a five-year-old merger of two parish communities. One had been a tony neighborhood parish with many professionals and a large school. The other had been a working-class parish that closed because airport expansion required the land.

The merger was ill-fit, and complex feelings remained close to the surface. The merger pastor's sensibilities were oriented toward a smiling but steam-rolling politics of unity and raising money to make it all happen. He left a year and a half after the merger. A green pastor replaced him. Young, handsome, and kind, he was popular. However, he evaded supervising staff, hung loose about finances, and was lackadaisical about the liturgy and faith formation. He served three years. His successor walked into a two-million-dollar debt, a half-million-dollar deficit, significant overstaffing in a shrinking school, a weak catechetical program, and casual liturgy. He decided to invite parish leadership and the community to planning.

Here, too, the beliefs statements composing and prioritizing process began a transformation of minds and hearts and deepened parish-wide communion in purpose. The beliefs statements, the values the community truly held, indicate the directional change.

BELIEFS STATEMENTS

✸ Our reverent celebration of Sunday Eucharist is the foundation of our parish community life.

✸ Our liturgical life, done with grace and devotion day by day, sustains our parish life and our communion with the worldwide Church.

✸ We pass on our faith life through our commitment to religious formation opportunities for people of all ages, circumstances, and backgrounds.

✸ We are committed in justice to be good stewards of our resources—money, property, and talents—for building up the common good.

✸ We value the participation and gifts of all in our parish community.

✸ A committed Christian spiritual life calls us to support one another toward becoming what we are called to be before God.

✸ Communicating with mutual respect and acceptance will lead us to justice and truth in our life together.

✸ We believe the Gospel calls us to recognize and respond to the needs of others.

✸ We are committed to a quality school grounded in Gospel ministry, solid academics in the Catholic liberal arts tradition, respect for the dignity of the human person, and parish life.

In Sum

The potential power of a highly participative beliefs statement composition and prioritizing process—pastoral leadership and parishioners listening, dialoguing, and coming to consensus about the common values the community holds—cannot be overestimated. The structured process of articulating common values, purpose, and function—identity—as a parish offers a community the opportunity to open eyes afresh, pry minds wide, fire hearts in warmth, and walk through new doors as the process explores the parish's deepest desires and its sense of the unique contribution it can make to the universal Gospel mission. ∎

A SAMPLE PASTORAL PLANNING PROCESS

Step 2: Parish Image

CLARIFY OUR COMMUNITY'S IMAGE: WHAT CONDITIONS PARISH ACTIVITY?

Step 2: Describing Parish Resources and Constraints

A. CHART THE PARISH'S ORGANIZATIONAL STRUCTURES

This step typically begins with the pastor sharing the parish organizational chart. If the parish does not have a complete and accurate diagram, then one needs to be made.

This task is complicated. Most likely, the planning group will immediately face the thorny question: does the provided material mirror reality? Often, the chart fails the test. Since the organizational chart represents power distribution in the parish, being ruthlessly honest about how power is really distributed—formally and informally—is necessary for the chart to serve planning and the parish. The group may need to plot several charts to truly understand how parish power distribution works. Being honest may then lead parish leaders toward this question: how do we *want* power distributed in the parish? The answer to that question can draw the planners into discussion about perceived problems and, hopefully, a wholesome structuring of parish power distribution.

The result of the process, however many sessions it may take—from two to four typically—should be a clean chart that represents real power distribution in the parish: healthy, accurate, and accountable. If the current reality is messy and unclear, revising power distribution to make it healthy would render this element of planning highly successful.

B. DESCRIBE BASIC POLICIES

Parishes pile up policies. This exercise gathers a specific set of policies, in writing or informal, limiting decisions by those who make policy. These would be policies that cannot be changed or violated without shifting the nature of the organization.

Questions that lead toward the completion of this task might be these:

* What are the extent and limits of the pastor's policymaking authority?

* What are the extent and limits of administrative staff members' and pastoral staff members' policymaking authority?

* What are the extent and limits of other parish groups' and organizations' authority to make policy?

Answering such questions may expose unnecessary overlap, some overreach, some meddling, and some holes. Exploring this reality allows for renewed clarity in decision-making: creating new freedoms, correcting misunderstandings, and easing relationships all around... or uncovering where unsettledness shall ever remain.

The illuminating result of these two to three sessions of work should be a clear and clean articulation of where policymaking authority, responsibility, accountability, and limits begin and end among all parish leaders.

C. DESCRIBE THE PARISH'S MAIN CHARACTERISTICS

The planning group then lists the identifying traits of the parish: its neighborhood, demographics, economics, size, contextual ministry commitments, contextual ministry limits, and its unique bends and twists because of its history.

This two-to-three-session exercise is often fun for the planning group. U.S. Census data markedly helps this exercise. At the same time, the effort requires storytelling. The major parish stories and talk around them typically clarifies the peculiar contours of the gifts and the stresses that make the parish what it is. The 30-year first pastorate, the historically inferior feelings of one of the parishes in the merger, the tenure of the priest later accused of sexual abuse, the fire… these events may have strongly shaped the parish's life. Their impact may demand reflection and frank assessment. The stories need to be told.

The result should be a clear listing of the elements that give the parish its unique personality, strengths, and limits.

D. DESIGNATE WHAT CHARACTERISTICS ARE STRENGTHS AND WEAKNESSES

First mark "+" next to positive characteristic. Then mark "-" for negative characteristics and "+/-" for neutral or mixed evaluations.

F. DESCRIBE ENVIRONMENTAL FACTORS THAT IMPACT THE PARISH.

This exercise aims to articulate the contextual, extrinsic factors that influence parish life over which it has no control.

Elements of this listing would include the economic health or stagnation of the city or neighborhood, perhaps the ideological posture of the bishop or clergy, the neighborhood's access to services, demographic trends, etc. For example: Holy Spirit, a neighborhood parish with others nearby, was split by a major thoroughfare. Christ the King was split by a creek bed where city homeless people lived in tents. St. Olaf sits in the middle of downtown, a bustling business community during the day and a disparate community of wandering street people at night and on weekends. St. Agnes has a long history of serving traditionalists city-wide. St. Joan of Arc has a long history of serving liberal discontents city-wide. The All Holy Angels merger has 600 families at five sites: the largest and youngest parish sits in a desert tourist town, the oldest parish sits in a small ranching community, one mission is in logging country, one in a rural community, and one in a part-time, developing ski area. The cathedral and chancery office are 300 miles away.

The results of this two-to-three-session element of the process should be a clear picture of the "givens" that identify the parish's ministry opportunities and limits and its call.

G. DESCRIBE PRESENT ASSUMPTIONS ABOUT THE PARISH'S FUTURE.

This exercise aims to articulate problems taken for granted in planning but problems that cannot be predicted by logical processes and that are beyond control. The planners might consider such concerns as these:

✽ Does Mass attendance or participation in RE programs seem to be growing or receding?

✽ How large and accessible, or small and inaccessible, seems the pool of lay ministers the parish needs to lead worship, catechesis, or pastoral care for the future?

✽ Does it look like the town's economic engine steel mill might close?

✽ Do the diocesan offices seem to be taking a long turn toward being more demanding yet less engaged?

✽ Might lay parish leaders be in this community's future?

✽ Might the city eventually look to build transitional housing for people experiencing homelessness on open land within the parish's boundaries?

The results of this two-to-three-session exchange should list eight to 15 cautionary factors that most parishioners would agree might be on the horizon and are to be taken for granted in planning for the future.

Share… Then Listen and Dialogue

All the above activities and resulting material are more fully informed and richly broadened when the planning group shares the process and its results with parish leadership and the parish assembly. Asking for feedback, observations, and input throughout the process draws the parish's image more accurately as it deepens the community's experience of itself as church. ∎

A SAMPLE PASTORAL PLANNING PROCESS

Sample Organizational Charts

A Parish as Corporation Sole

Accurate according to canon law, this chart might be modified for a parish on the synodal way. The modification might be overlapping among the pastor, councils, pastoral staff. The solid and dashed lines might also be reconsidered. Note: the outer circle is the parish Christifideles.

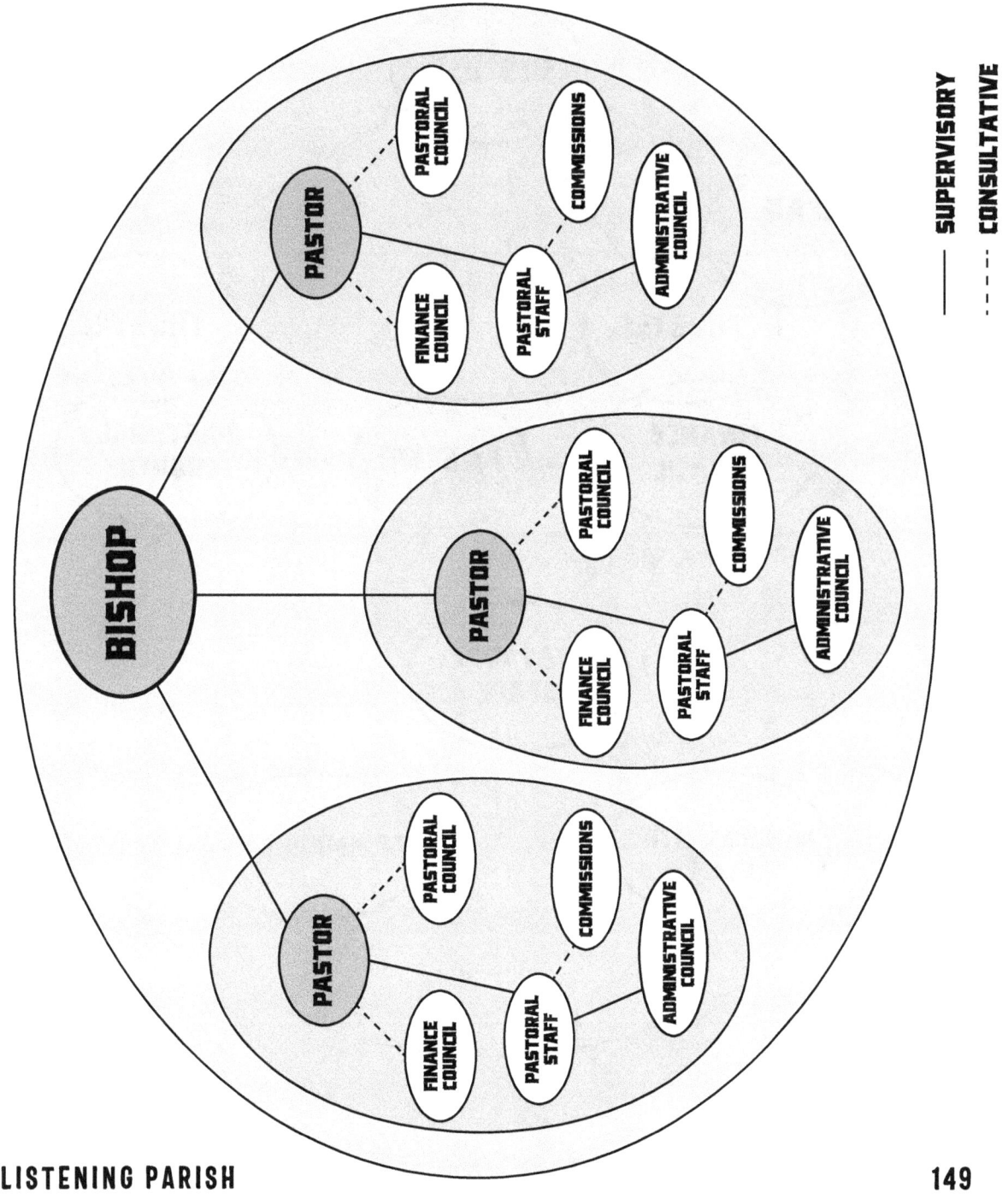

THE LISTENING PARISH

A Parish as Independent Corporation

Accurate according to canon law, for a parish on the synodal way, this chart might be modified into more overlapping among the pastor, councils, and staff. The solid and dashed lines might also be reconsidered. Note: the outer circle represents the Christifideles of the parish.

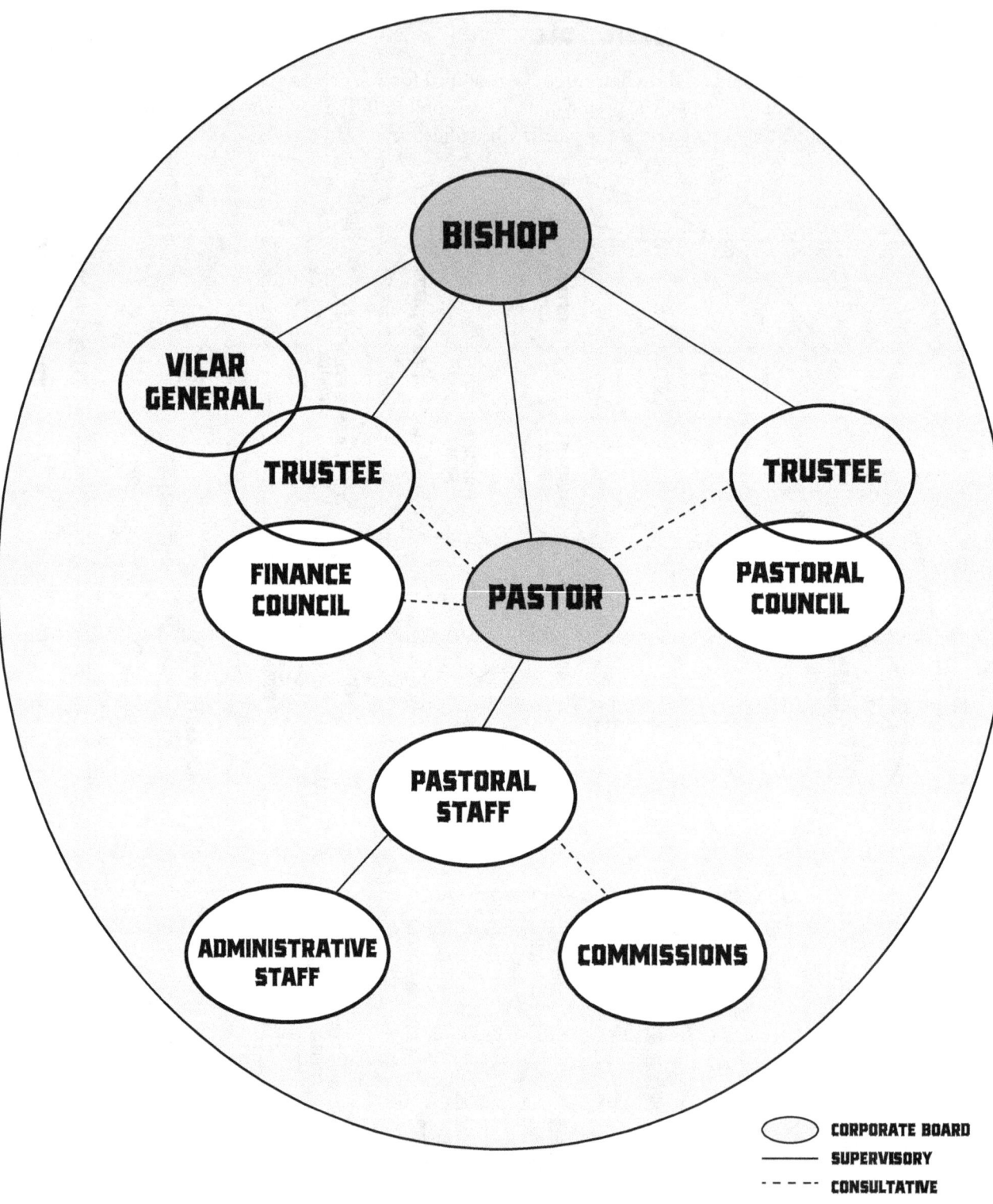

A SAMPLE PASTORAL PLANNING PROCESS

Step 3: Parish Direction

ARTICULATING OUR COMMUNITY'S DIRECTION, WHAT WE INTEND TO DO

This element of the planning process represents a turning point because it attempts to describe the parish in terms of what it aspires to be.

STEP 3: Formulate Goals and Objectives.

A. ESTABLISH GENERAL THREE-YEAR OR FIVE-YEAR GOALS.

The planning group then formulates quantitative or qualitative statements that express, in broad terms, what the parish intends to achieve over the next three to five years. The goals represent the parish's continuing intention for the next period.

The goals best comprise major desires of and for the parish's becoming more itself. They are listed in priority. Goals represent the guiding aims of the parish's energy and resources—within or in addition to its constant ministry commitment—for the coming years. A goal could be moving toward adding a staff member, gradually moving the school community toward paying full-cost tuition, improving the quality of the liturgical music program, purchasing a building for the pastor's living quarters, completing a full census of the parish, etc. The matter for the goals ought to be major efforts that will shape the community more effectively for its pastoral mission and draw it forward in that mission.

The result should be a list of four or five goals that the parish aims to accomplish in an agreed-upon period, typically five years.

B. ESTABLISH SPECIFIC OBJECTIVES.

Under each goal, the planning group writes out, in logical order, specific activities that represent a partial realization of the continuing goal.

This exercise requires logical thinking and a practical sense of the progression of activities necessary for accomplishing the goal with a dash of creativity. Establishing objectives for each goal should take three sessions for composing and revising until the group feels comfortable with the result. Three sessions, some time spent on each set of objectives during each meeting, should accomplish the task.

The result should be a listing of six to nine achievable objectives under each goal, discreet activities that mark a step toward achieving the goal. ■

A SAMPLE PASTORAL PLANNING PROCESS

Sample Goals & Objectives

The following represents one parish's progression through the planning process.

Note the priority of the goals. Goal four represents a facilities review that may move the parish toward a major construction project and financial outlay. The objectives underneath goal four also delineate more extended and complex activities than the other goals. Indeed, the parish eventually did build. Nonetheless, the consensus of the planning group in consultation with the parish assembly set the goals' priority as concerns of belonging, ministry evaluation and accountability, and ongoing communication.

Through the spiritually based planning process, despite aching facilities needs, the parish planners and assembly discerned that major ministry concerns required priority over the excitement of erecting facilities.

GOAL I

Establish experiences that will deepen a sense of belonging in the parish community.

Primary Responsibility:

❋ Faith Formation Commission

❋ Pastoral Care Commission

Objectives:

❋ Assess needs, expectations, and opportunities for belonging.

❋ Establish a process for developing small faith communities.

❋ Establish experiences that specifically study and help us improve our parish life, particularly in relationship to:

  1. welcoming,
  2. hospitality,
  3. social opportunities, and
  4. outreach to those who feel alienated, people with disabilities, or those from diverse backgrounds.

GOAL II

Develop a process of assessment and accountability in all areas of ministry.

Primary Responsibility:

❋ Pastoral Council

Objectives:

❋ Establish a commission in each area of ministry to focus, guide, and monitor parish ministries.

❋ Formulate a mission statement for each ministry.

❋ Establish a process of annual goal-setting for all parish ministries. This process may include: definition of ministry needs/priorities, the methods of obtaining parishioner input, goals statements, and implementation/evaluation plans.

❋ Establish a process for the review of ministry goals and mission statement (at least annually).

❋ Establish a process for communicating goals and results to parishioners.

GOAL III

Develop a strategy to assess parish communications to improve their effectiveness.

Primary responsibility:

❋ Parish Council

Objectives:

❋ Examine what needs to be communicated and by whom.

❋ Examine current methods of relaying information (i.e., financial information, notification of events, projects, etc.) to parishioners.

❋ Examine current methods to share formational and/or educational information with parishioners.

❋ Develop a plan for the use of multiple approaches for communicating all information to insure broad and effective dissemination.

❋ Examine current linkages between parish leadership groups and develop a plan to ensure effective communication among all leadership groups.

❋ Examine current methods of obtaining input from parishioners.

❋ Develop a plan that provides opportunities for parishioners to ask questions and have them answered, raise issues and have them addressed, and give feedback to parish leadership and receive an appropriate response.

GOAL IV

Develop a strategic plan for the assessment, development, and expansion of facilities in service of parish ministries.

Primary responsibility:

❋ Finance Council

Objectives:

❋ Conduct a feasibility study that will consider changes in parish properties and operations.

❋ Assess the desire and ability of the parish community to commit to daycare ministry and establish an appropriate facility.

❋ Assess the desire and ability of the school ministry to make changes in properties and operations.

❋ Assess the desire and commitment of the parish community to commit to the programs and upkeep that would be necessary for a parish gymnasium.

❋ Review the structural quality of current facilities and the technical issues relating to any changes in current properties or operations.

❋ Assess the ability of the parish to expand and maintain its ministries.

❋ Study all financial issues relative to any changes in parish properties and operations.

❋ Establish a process for demonstrating parish-wide personal and financial support for any proposed changes.

❋ Determine the use of any new facilities and oversee their design.

❋ Lead the community in completing any changes in ministries, properties, and operations. ■

A SAMPLE PASTORAL PLANNING PROCESS

Steps 4-8. Parish Accomplishment

ACCOMPLISHMENT: ARTICULATING HOW WE ARE GOING TO DO IT

For the planning group, the purpose of these exercises is to provide helpful suggestions and guideposts for measuring progress through the planning process. Designated responsible persons and groups further develop and inform what the planning group provides.

Step 4: Collect data on the intended objectives and analyze trends.

A. COLLECT NECESSARY DATA FOR ACCOMPLISHING THE GOALS.

The planning group needs to gather the pertinent facts as an information base for beginning the planning work and measuring its relative success.

The result should be a packet accompanying the goals and objectives that equips the people responsible for the next planning steps with all the information at hand to accomplish their part of the process.

B. ANALYZE TRENDS THAT IMPACT ACCOMPLISHING THE GOAL.

The planning group needs to establish the general lines of development to accomplish the objectives and project these lines into the future.

The result should be a listing of projected tasks/activities under each objective with a likely time allotment for accomplishing each. This listing offers those responsible for the next steps a helpful sense of the terrain the planners expect to cover and the time frame for accomplishing each objective.

C. NOTE PLANNING GAPS.

Based on the data collection and trend analysis, and before commissioning the next steps to those responsible, the planning group needs to fill whatever gaps it has come to see in the process because of missed data, a change in environmental factors, the exposure of faulty assumptions, or emerging intractable difficulties.

The result should be tweaking or revision of the goals, objectives, data, and trends analysis that will very practically help the implementers of the next steps of the process to accomplish their objectives and thus the goals.

Step 5: Design programs to achieve the objectives.

A. ESTABLISH GENERAL STRATEGIES FOR ACCOMPLISHING EACH GOAL.

The planning group develops guidelines for what the apt and helpful resources—materials, workshops, travel, consultations, methods, etc.—will likely be to achieve the objectives.

The result should be a listing attached to the objectives and projected tasks/activities that offers tips, cues, and options for making the next steps effective and efficient: further data development, practically shaping the work and accomplishing the objective.

B. DESIGN ALTERNATIVE PROGRAMS AS BACKUP POSSIBILITIES.

The planning group needs to weigh and share various proposed options for possible approaches to accomplish the objectives effectively.

The result should be added notes of options under the activities/tasks of each objective. The notes might be formulated as proposed projects.

C. ASSIGN ACTION RESPONSIBILITY FOR ACCOMPLISHING THE GOALS AND OBJECTIVES.

The planning group assigns a particular person or group responsibility for each planning action or program implementation expected or proposed during the accomplishment of the objectives and goals. This step requires consultation with each proposed responsible person or group and their consent to perform their role. This listening and dialogue ought to include cost projections.

The result should be an assigned responsible person or group—staff and other parish leaders—for every task/activity under each objective, every objective under each goal, and every goal.

Step 6: Allocate the necessary resources.

A. DO A BUDGETARY ANALYSIS AND ESTIMATE THE NEEDED RESOURCES.

The group determines the likely cost of completing the goals and objectives over five years.

The result will be budget proposals for the subsequent years that will be submitted to the pastor, pastoral council, and finance council. The proposals would also be shared with persons or groups responsible for accomplishing objectives for their budget process.

B. ALLOCATE RESOURCES.

This task belongs to the pastor, parish staff, councils, and other leadership groups.

Step 7: Coordinate and schedule activities to achieve the objectives.

This step belongs to those persons assigned responsibility in the planning document for accomplishing the goals, objectives, and activities/tasks underneath them.

This extended step should include the planning group meeting—together or separately—with each person or group assigned an objective to accomplish and some of those assigned an activity/task, depending. The meeting would be to develop expectations, clarify concerns, modify processes, adjust timelines, modify the budget, be made aware of people whose responsibilities also require participation, and keep informed, etc.

Step 8: Review and evaluate programs regarding the intended objectives and recycle the results.

This step builds in co-responsibility and accountability. Both the planning group and those responsible for execution of the plan benefit from regular listening and dialogue about progress toward the objectives and activities/tasks. This communication exchange helps everyone grow in mutual understanding and accountability, grapple with how to share progress with parish leadership groups and the parish assembly, and develop an overall appreciation of the entire planning effort and the ins, outs, ups, and downs of its accomplishment.

Dialogue and listening—planners and implementers together, discerning in an ongoing way how to include the entire parish and the peripheries—enable the ongoing modification, revision, and expansion of the objectives or the goals as everyone proceeds through the process.

Specifics!

The whole plan is ideally articulated as concretely as possible, mindful that its progress will offer the planning group and those responsible for the objectives and activities/tasks, not to mention parish leadership and the parish assembly, abundant calls for modification.

And Then...

In the end, the planning group and parish leadership offer the parish assembly full accountability for the whole process. After listening and dialoguing together—parish leadership and the parish assembly—the whole process begins again.

PARISH SYNODALITY IN PRACTICE

PARISH SYNODALITY IN PRACTICE

Living the Spirit of Synodality

The Invitation of Synodality

Synodality practices aim to help a parish incarnate in our time and place the radically inclusive ministry of Jesus Christ. They invite all participants to receive the mercy of God, express that mercy, and extend it.

Mercy

The Latin word for mercy is *misericordia*. Its etymology carries the twofold connotation of wretchedness (*miseria*, misery) and love (*cor*, heart).

Pope Francis wrote about mercy in his November 2016 apostolic exhortation:

> Mercy is love responding to misery; it is misery calling forth love. An attribute of God, mercy is compassion and love shown towards those who have no claim to expect or receive kindness.
>
> Pope Francis, *Misericordia et Misera*

Jesuit Father James Keenan summarizes mercy's meaning pointedly: "the willingness to enter into the chaos of another."

Synodality Practice's Focus: The Ministry of Mercy

The pastoral ministry toward which synodality aims is to do as Jesus did, to extend God's mercy. Thus, the fundamental questions underneath synodality practice, especially as we reach toward the peripheries, are these:

✸ What does it mean for me, for us, to enter into the chaos of this person's or this group's life?

✸ What does the call to mercy demand of me now, in this situation?

While asking these questions, synodality practice invites us as church to listen, dialogue, discern, take decisions, and implement and evaluate them... in the process of being and becoming church more fully.

Synodality practices serve a parish's call, the Church's call, and the Gospel's call to be a people who distinguish ourselves by our willingness to enter the chaos of other people's lives.

Incarnating Radical Inclusion to Those on the Peripheries

The possibilities empowered through synodality practices build hope. These practices enable the

THE LISTENING PARISH

Christifideles, the people of God, to proclaim with our lives that no one is excluded from God's mercy.

That is, synodality practices ignite for the parish the possibility that we, the Christifideles, the people of God, will recognize that we have nothing to fear by engaging, like Jesus did, every form of human misery—addiction, promiscuity, depression, violence, abandonment, mental illness, sexual dysphoria, poverty, homelessness, loneliness, sickness, handicap, abuse, loss, grief, physical suffering. What is required of us is that we give ourselves over to the Spirit's power.

Incarnating Our Own Radical Being Included

Synodal practices equip faithful people to find practical ways to offer Jesus' love and life to all those burdened with misery. That is, they push us to proclaim with our words and acts that no one is excluded from extending mercy.

Thus, through its synodality practices, a parish, the Church, reaches for the participation of all in common mission, even those to and for whom we seek to extend mercy.

Following the Pattern of Life Jesus Showed Us

Synodal practice calls the Church to be radiant in the midst of the world as the mercy seat of Christ's radically inclusive love and the empowered-by-the-Spirit field hospital whose mission is to offer mercy to the world.

> I dream of a "missionary option," that is, a missionary impulse capable of transforming everything, so that the Church's customs, ways of doing things, times and schedules, language and structures can be suitably channeled for the evangelization of today's world rather than for her self-preservation.
>
> Pope Francis, *Joy of the Gospel*, 27

The Hope of the Christifideles

We the Church listen, dialogue, discern, take decisions, implement them, and evaluate them so we might experience Jesus' all-inclusive love and mercy ourselves and so that we might extend Jesus' radical mercy and radical inclusion to all humans everywhere.

Thus, the practical aim of synodality practice is to extend hope, joy, and life to the ends of the earth, seeking to heal and transform the world in faithfulness to our Gospel mission. ■

PARISH SYNODALITY IN PRACTICE

Some Limits

Remaining One in the Body of Christ

Participation, communion, ongoing conversion in conformity to Christ, accompanying those in need (especially the poor), and evangelization—these are the aims of synodality practices.

Synodality practices, however, expose limits. Three points deserve brisk mention.

Moreover, the Church itself circumscribes and limits the possibilities of synodality. In that connection, two points are noteworthy.

Limits Exposed by the Practices

The first noteworthy limit is simply that the processes of synodality demand choices. To say yes to extending mercy on one level or in a particular instance means that 30 concerns may be addressed only partially, and 100 others may not be addressed at all.

Implementing synodality practices, therefore, includes reaching a discernment consensus about priorities. Though it is constituent to being Church in the parish, that can be a bracing process.

The second limit is that, for all the efforts, methods, and means employed in engaging participation, some pastoral leaders, some in the parish assembly, and some among those on the peripheries will not or cannot participate. Every effort must always be made to include everyone in the process so the Spirit can move among us. The principles of synodality practice demand that. Nonetheless, the process will require letting go of some potential participants. That, too, though painful, is a spiritual part of the process: surrendering to reality.

The third limit is that methods, ways, and means will fail. At this time in the life of the Church, experimentation is inherent in implementing synodality practices. Not all will work. Maybe even most will fail.

What's important is trying again, reaching for what works, and sharing the experience as widely as possible.

Any parish attempting to implement synodality practices faces these limits.

The Nature of the Church Limits Synodality Dynamics

In the early decades after Christ, the Christian Way spread through the founding of supper clubs across the Mediterranean basin.

Provocative and clumsy as this notion may seem, that is precisely the conclusion of the 2021 book *After Jesus Before Christianity*, edited for the Westar Christianity Seminar by the scholars Erin Vearncombe, Brandon Scott, and Hal Taussig. This conclusion has wide-ranging and gritty implications for synodality.

Pope Francis refers to parishes, diocesan churches, and the universal Church as a community of communities. Beautiful as that may be to contemplate, one stimulating angle on that observation is to reflect on the simple fact that the Church is also a club of clubs.

That is, sociologically, the Church has always been a closed group. It admits only initiates who have completed certain requirements and ritual steps. Its inner life is enjoyed only by the initiated. Its leaders hold unique and extraordinary power. Its rules are binding and enforced. Violation of rules can lead to separation and exclusion.

Not only is the Church a club, but so are its constituent parts. The bishops are a club, priests are a club, deacons are a club, the whole clergy is a club. The Roman Curia is a club, the cardinals are a club, a church province is a club, a diocese is a club. A parish is also a club, and a club of clubs.

This club dynamic, though real, ought not to be pressed too hard.

Nonetheless, this club dynamic suggests why the implementation of synodality practices—radically inclusive, opposed to exclusion of any sort—threatens members of the club(s). This club-breaking dynamic also suggests the enormity of change afoot in the Church today and the likelihood that the going will be rough, slow, and protracted.

These dynamics need to be acknowledged straightforwardly.

In the Church, Authority Is Held Close

Though the movement today, sparked by Pope Francis and venerable in the Tradition, is to implement synodality practices on all levels of the Church—universal, continental, national, regional, and diocesan—every level holds close and tight its decision-making and action-taking authority.

This holding close demands that each level of the Church remain aware, within synodality practice, of what decisions it may or may not make and what actions it may or may not take.

Response to the German Synodal Way stands out as an example of how nervous and defensive authority can be if it feels threatened by what it sees as crossing boundaries. Pope Francis continues to support the German Synodal Way. He has, however, called it elitist. The Vatican and some among the world bishops have warned the Germans about the authority their process does not have and the lines it ought not to cross. Fearful of fracture—or loss of control?—they call the German Church to remain in concord with the Church Universal. Some bishops have advocated that the Vatican shut the process down.

One rule of thumb: the aim of synodality practices is communion in ongoing listening, dialogue, discernment, and pastoral transformation, not doctrinal change.

Pope Francis allows for the possibility of practice and doctrinal emphasis change over extended time as consensus builds. That, however, will be a matter discerned by the Bishop of Rome and the college of bishops, not the continental, regional, provincial, or diocesan churches… nor the parish.

These dynamics, too, need to be straightforwardly acknowledged and understood. ■

PARISH SYNODALITY IN PRACTICE

Participation in God's Family Life

The Synodal Life of the Trinity

To the right, you see a stimulating and accessible image of God: the 15th-century Russian icon by Andrei Rublev entitled Trinity. A treasure trove of meaning, the icon proclaims not only that our God is a community of persons but also offers us the flavor of that community relationship as it depicts the Trinity in table fellowship.

The icon shows the Father, Son, and Holy Spirit bound together in listening and dialogue, in participation, co-responsibility, and communion... as a family.

The Family Life of God

LISTENING AND DIALOGUE IN COMMUNION AND PARTICIPATION

The thrones, scepters, and royal footstools depict the Trinity's bond in equal dignity. All have the same countenance (identity). All are winged (otherworldly). All wear celestial blue (abiding in the heavenly realms). These similarities tell us of their mutuality in life together. The personal focus of each on the other illustrates their interdependence and common bond.

If you allow your eyes to follow from the far shoulder of the figure on the left, down to the feet, then across to the feet of the figure on the right, then up that figure's body to the shoulder and across the tops of the figures' heads—the whole image bends in this way—you see that the Trinity sits in a perfect circle, proclaiming its absolute communion in relationship.

The androgyny of the figures proclaims that same unity. The halo on each proclaims their common holiness. The right hand extended in blessing proclaims their common mission.

THE LISTENING PARISH

The cup of wine in the center of the low table around which they sit, symbol of the new covenant in Christ's blood we and they share, depicts the joy the Trinity experiences in life together.

DIVERSITY AND COMPLEMENTARY IN MISSION

The dress of the three figures—the Father on the left robed in light, the Son in the center robed in his two natures of earthy blood red and heavenly blue, the Holy Spirit on the right robed in the vital green of hope and life—announces their distinctness in mission.

The temple behind the Father, the tree of life behind the Son, and the mountain behind the Holy Spirit (on which in the End Time the 144,000 assemble whose robes are washed clean in the blood of the Lamb) also accent the particularity of each within the mission of all.

Invited to Share the Trinity's Family Life

This image invites us as onlookers to participate in the transcendent, eternal communion and diversity in mission that is the Trinity's own life.

Look at the figures' eyes!

The Son, who presides over the Trinity's life—"Everything that the Father has is mine," Jesus says at the end of Matthew's Gospel, "All authority in heaven and on earth has been given to me"—gazes upon the Father, the origin of all life.

The Father, the beautiful one ever ancient, ever new, who "established the heavens" (Proverbs 8:27), gazes across the table to the Spirit, whom the Father sends forth.

The Holy Spirit, "from of old… poured forth, at the first, before the earth" (Proverbs 8:23), gazes to the open space at table in the center of the icon.

That open space upon which the Holy Spirit gazes is the place at table left for us. The Spirit looks to this open place in invitation, bidding us to join the Trinity in their table fellowship, to participate with the Trinity in its divine life.

The Aim of God's Life and Ours

The aim of God's divine life is love and justice. In love, the Trinity calls us to tender care and self-emptying service. In justice, the Trinity calls us to freedom, security, and the fulfillment of one another's need—right ordering in our relationships.

Within their transcendent, eternal participation and communion, the Father, Son, and Holy Spirit extend inclusive love and merciful justice to one another perfectly.

Whenever we extend others' oppression instead of freedom, insecurity instead of security, or want instead of fulfilling their need—un-love and injustice—then we withdraw from table fellowship with the Trinity. We are extending to others what is opposed to the Trinity's life, and we sin.

Accepting the Spirit's Invitation

We the Church accept the Spirit's invitation to join in the Trinity's own life whenever we express communion in reciprocal listening and dialogue, participate together in our common life and common mission, and exercise our diverse gifts co-responsibly while speaking and acting in communion.

When we share the divine life through our synodal practice, we live out our God-given unity and distinctness in mission for God, the Church, and the world.

ABOUT THE AUTHOR

MICHAEL L. PAPESH was ordained in 1983 and is now retired from active ministry. He has served as campus minister, parochial vicar, weekend assistant, principal, CRE, and pastor; in seminary spiritual formation at the undergraduate and graduate school levels; on numerous diocesan committees and boards related to priestly life and ministry; and in diocesan chancery ministry.

He has a B.A. in English from St. Meinrad College, master's degrees from Indiana University and St. Meinrad School of Theology, and a Doctor of Ministry degree from United Theological Seminary of the Twin Cities. He is also the author of *Clerical Culture: Contradiction and Transformation* from Liturgical Press and *Good News Parish Leadership* from Twenty-Third Publications, as well as articles on clerical culture and liturgical presiding. He has won two Catholic Press Association Awards. Papesh has also won four literary awards after publishing two memoirs.

www.ingramcontent.com/pod-product-compliance
Lightning Source LLC
Chambersburg PA
CBHW080436230426
43662CB00015B/2284